RILEY HERN

E. PAYAN

WALTER SMAILL

J. HALL

GORDON ROBERT

FRED TAYLOR

JOE MALONE

D. PITRE

MARTY WALSH

JACK LAVIOLETTE of Canadian Club

ARTHUR ROSS

HAMBY SHORE

COBALT

# HOCKEY

## THE ILLUSTRATED HISTORY

1963

# HOCKEY
## THE ILLUSTRATED HISTORY

An official publication of the
National Hockey League

Text by Charles Wilkins

Edited by Dan Diamond

Doubleday Canada Limited, Toronto, Canada
Doubleday & Company, Inc., Garden City, New York

1985

Library of Congress Catalog Card Number: 85-15924

**HOCKEY**
**THE ILLUSTRATED HISTORY**
©1985 by Dan Diamond and Peter McGoey

Produced by Dan Diamond and Associates Inc.

Designed by Steve Manley, Overleaf Design Ltd.

Production by Paula Chabanais Productions

Typesetting by Stars & Type Inc.

Canadian cataloging in publication data
Diamond, Dan
    Hockey, the illustrated history

Includes index.
ISBN 0-385-23329-9
1. National Hockey League — History. I. Wilkins, Charles. II. Title.
GV847.8.N37D53 1985      796.96'2'06      C85-099253-2

Library of Congress cataloging in publication data
Diamond, Dan
    Hockey, the illustrated history

    Includes index.
    1. National Hockey League — History. I. Wilkins, Charles. II. Title.
GV847.8.N3D53 1985      796.96'2'09      85-15924
ISBN 0-385-23329-9

Doubleday Canada Limited, Toronto, Canada
Doubleday & Company, Inc., Garden City, New York

Printed in Canada by John Deyell Company
10 9 8 7 6 5 4 3 2

In fond memory of
Foster William Hewitt
whose exceptional voice linked us
to the excitement of the game

# HOCKEY

c. 1955

c. 1955

# INTRODUCTION

Every Christmas, thousands upon thousands of youngsters open presents containing hockey equipment. Many of them dream, for an instant, of playing in the National Hockey League. In June each year, the NHL conducts its annual entry draft of about 240 hockey players old enough and talented enough to be considered for spots on the rosters of its teams. And, later, in September, the league holds a ceremony in which three retired hockey players are inducted into the Hockey Hall of Fame. That's quite a winnowing process: thousands upon thousands finally reduced to three.

When you see a modern hockey player skate out to take the opening face-off in an NHL hockey game, he represents much more than 200 pounds of trained athlete. He personifies success. He's someone who has almost always made the team. He's passed from the thousands upon thousands to the 240 and beyond.

But he also runs the risk of being identified with failure. He's there to win the face-off, the game, the season, the playoffs and the bigger battle against time. In all of these confrontations, the odds are no better than even. In most, they're considerably worse. And fifteen thousand patrons in the arena have purchased the right to be critical of his play.

He is also a testament to luck. He's been lucky to stay healthy, lucky to have played well while being scouted and lucky to be drafted by a team that needs his particular skills.

He embodies sacrifice. The training, the physical punishment and the support of his family and minor-hockey coaches all had to be there in order for this moment to take place.

He stands for tradition. His energies are focused on winning the Stanley Cup, an outsized silver bowl donated long ago by the Queen's own representative to the Dominion of Canada. The Cup itself isn't perfect; it has its share of dents, and the engravings of hundreds of hockey players' names on its surface are curiously irregular. But to our hockey player, it is perfection itself. He lives to be part of a Stanley Cup-winning team, to know that his name joins the Taylors, Nighbors, Morenzes, Richards, Howes, Orrs and Gretzkys inscribed on the shiny barrel of the trophy.

1958

**Four hockey greats** sit for portraits that are on permanent display in the Hockey Hall of Fame. From left: Red Dutton, Lester Patrick, Al Pickard and George Dudley. Dutton and Patrick were fine players; all four were enthusiastic builders of the sport.

He represents progress, too, in a sport that has never stopped changing. The rules of the game, the speed at which it's played, the methods of the player's coach and the equipment he wears are all part of a continual evolution.

Throughout 100 years of organized hockey, the stars of one era can never be fairly evaluated against those of any other. Would Wayne Gretzky have made the difference for the team from Rat Portage against the Ottawa Silver Seven in the 1905 Stanley Cup final? Who knows? The question is absurd. Perhaps, if Gretzky had grown up in the nineteenth century, the combination of poor diet and harsh living conditions wouldn't have allowed Wayne's father to prepare his promising youngster for future stardom. Could Russell Bowie have made the 1960 Canadiens' lineup? His numbers look impressive: 234 goals in 80 games. That's fantastic. But, Bowie's 80 games took place between 1899 and 1908. They certainly weren't packed into the six months of a single NHL regular season. On top of that, Mr. Bowie weighed a mere 112 pounds — not quite up to the heftiness of today's professional standard.

Hockey fans and commentators have always labeled the period immediately preceding the current one in the sport's development as a

"Golden Age." Today, the pre-expansion years of the 1950s and '60s have acquired this luster. After the war, it was the '30s that were similarly revered. In 1943, many felt the game was ruined by the adoption of the center redline. And in the 1920s, longtime fans lamented the advent of unrestricted forward passing as needless tampering that was sure to spoil the sport. Years later, these fears seem almost amusing. When you look at hockey from the 1880s until today, one thing is clear: it's all one game that gripped its fanciers with the same fascination then as now.

From a chilly enclosed rink in a turn-of-the-century mining boom-town, to a modern super-arena in a big city, we have always been drawn to those moments when the players do something that we recognize is one notch faster, harder, smoother, tougher or more stylish than we can do ourselves.

It doesn't always happen this way. Not every team is a winner, not every moment inspired. But when it works — when the common will of the team brings forth a splendid effort from an individual player — the fan takes from hockey the greatest reward of enthusiasm: a reason for fervor and the inspiration to strive for the same kind of excellence in day-to-day affairs.

All this from a game.

*Hockey: The Illustrated History* is the result of the most comprehensive survey of hockey photography ever conducted. The story it tells picks from the best and brightest. Still, due to size limitations, it can't depict every significant contributor to a game that has sustained more than a century of growth and passionate involvement from its participants.

Those whose faces you don't see in this book are here nonetheless. They made the game of hockey worth depicting and writing about as surely as those whose images are recorded here.

*—Dan Diamond*

# THE MATCHLESS GIANTS

One night late in 1960, between Christmas and New Year's, my uncle Ralph and I got into his shiny Ford Galaxie 500 and drove from suburban east-end Toronto to a tiny backstreet near the intersection of Carlton and Parliament in the center of the city. We parked the car, walked out to Carlton and boarded a westbound streetcar. I was visiting Toronto for Christmas vacation and was unfamiliar with the city. Nonetheless, I knew that our destination, Maple Leaf Gardens, was somewhere in the distance ahead of us; and as we jounced and rattled along Carlton Street I kept my face pressed to the window, straining for a glimpse of the preeminent shrine of my boyhood. If it struck me as odd or time-consuming that we hadn't driven our entire route, I wasn't about to mention it; I had never seen an NHL game and my expectations were high enough that I would quite happily have walked, or crawled, to get to one – particularly one between the Toronto Maple Leafs, on whom my best hopes had risen and fallen for as long as I could remember (five years at most), and the current Stanley Cup champions, the enemy, the Montreal Canadiens.

As we got off the streetcar and were absorbed by the thousands converging on the Gardens, as we crowded in under the marquee and pushed through the turnstiles into the lobby, as we rode the escalator to the upper levels of the building, one passionate concern dominated my thoughts–that the Leafs should win the game. As far as I was concerned they *had* to win – if for no other reason than for me. I couldn't countenance any other result; I had followed them too long, invested so much, come so far.

My hopeful anticipation was far from unrealistic. The Leafs' nemesis of the past decade, the frightening Rocket Richard, had retired the previous spring; and Toronto's Frank Mahovlich had begun the season at a stupefying goal-scoring pace, impressing not only a devoted young Leafs supporter but a whole continent of hockey fans. By Christmas he

13

**Bill Barilko's glorious last moment** in the NHL won the 1951 Stanley Cup for the Toronto Maple Leafs. All five games in the finals went into overtime, this one ending 3-2.

had scored some 35 goals and for the past month had been locked in what seemed a Titanic struggle with Montreal's Bernie "Boom-Boom" Geoffrion for the lead in the league scoring race. Every day through December I had rushed home from school and grabbed the *Cornwall Standard Freeholder* and checked first the game scores from the previous night and second the summaries, to see whether Boom-Boom or Frank had gained points. A Mahovlich goal was enough to boost my spirits until the next game. A Geoffrion goal was a rude scar on the sports page.

The emotions and memories guard themselves in incontrovertible ways; and it is certainly a measure of my early passion for the Maple Leafs that, as I sat at my desk a few days ago, I could not remember whether they had won that night's game. A short walk to the library and a glance at the record books confirmed what I had suspected – that the Maple Leafs had lost and Mahovlich had not scored.

Yet, although I had forgotten, or had chosen to forget, the game's outcome, I remember distinctly almost everything else about the night: the sight of the Gardens' high, yellow walls; walking up the ramp and emerg-

c. 1948

**Rocket Richard played with an intensity** that carried him around, over or through opposing players. In his 18 big-league seasons he was thunder and lightning in the NHL. In this photo, the blade of his skate has shattered the "unbreakable" glass.

"I remember seeing this picture when I was a kid visiting Maple Leaf Gardens. It was that unbreakable glass that enforced the distance between us as kids and the Richards on the ice in the Gardens. We still had metal mesh in our rinks. The unbreakable glass, though this picture disproves that, was an unmistakable sign of the big leagues." — *Ken Dryden*

ing into the great bowl of seats that surrounds the ice (it seemed *impossible* that an arena could be that big); Red Kelly's bright orange hair (till then I had seen him only on black-and-white television; I remember how *expansive* the game seemed, free of the margins of my parents' old 21-inch Rogers Majestic. And how fast and dangerous it all was, and how the crash of a body check – that chilling percussion of pads and sticks – could be heard right up into the corner blues where I was sitting. And how at certain moments you could hear the players shouting to one another. I remember searching the rafters for Foster Hewitt's legendary "gondola", and appreciating what it was to witness the first period of a game, having for years seen only the second and third periods, the only periods broadcast at that time on *Hockey Night in Canada*. I remember the red-and-blue vividness of the uniforms, and how hundreds of men in the stands wore fedora hats, as they never did at the Cornwall Arena.

But what I recall as well as, or better than, anything is standing in the lower corridors and foyer, both before and after the game, gazing at the big framed photos that lined the walls. Two in particular grabbed my attention: the well-known depiction of Bill Barilko diving icewards as he scored the winning goal in the 1951 Stanley Cup finals, and the bizarre photo of Rocket Richard falling to the ice, his skate having crashed through the "unbreakable" glass at the end of the rink. What more in the way of fascination or theatrics could a pair of photos deliver to a 12-year-old boy? Yet what intrigued me about the Barilko photo was not just the spectacle of the image itself, or the awareness that the Stanley Cup had been won at precisely that moment, but the knowledge that the Leafs' hero had flown north on a fishing trip a short time after the photo had been taken and had never been seen again. That morbid and mysterious fact superimposed on the triumphal image of the goal being scored was about as much in the way of irony as my young mind could handle.

What intrigued me about the Richard photo was in a curious way related to the Barilko photo. I would not have seen the relation at the time, but, nonetheless, there in front of me was the evidence, utterly convincing to a child, that nothing was for sure, that the assumed order of things could not be taken for granted, that the "unbreakable" could be smashed. In a less metaphysical sense, the photo also happened to be a great piece of camera work.

I have been back to the Gardens many times since and cannot recall an occasion when I did not pause, however briefly, to glance at those photos.

## Photographic memories

Canadian writer George Morrissette once said that, for him, lacing on skates as an adult and going out on the neighborhood rink put him keenly in touch with a more innocent time of life. Inasmuch as the old hockey photos evoke the spirit in which we once pursued our heroes and obsessions, they, too, connect us to a more innocent version of ourselves. Indeed, those of us who were raised on the game of hockey would find it difficult to approach the vintage photos with anything other than the fascination, the untainted perceptions, of childhood.

This is not to say the photos are merely a key to our recollections and emotions. They are, above all, a vivid documentation of the emotions, hazards and minutiae of the game itself – of its dramatic moments as well as its mere trappings and equipment. They are a historic chronicle which, when read with precision, can provide an account as telling as that of any record book, collection of numbers, or written report. Their currency is not statistics or analysis, but theatre, pageantry and, at their most evocative, the raw emotions and spirit of the game. They recall not just

**Tough mining towns** took to hockey in the early days of the game. This match was played in Dawson City. 1900

individual players or moments, but games, seasons, teams and, in some cases, entire decades, careers, or eras of the sport.

Understandably, the further back we go in the history of the sport – the 1940s, '30s, '20s – the greater the difficulty in obtaining any variety of photographs. Relative to today, when mountains of photos of the superstars are in circulation, there are perhaps only two or three available shots of early stars such as Georges Vezina, Joe Malone or Cyclone Taylor. In the 30-odd years I have followed hockey, I can recall seeing only two photos of Howie Morenz whom many believe was the premier player of the first half of the century. I have seen hundreds, if not thousands, of photos of Wayne Gretzky, Mike Bossy and Darryl Sittler. It is all but impossible to walk by a Canadian newsstand these days, even at the height of summer, without seeing at least a couple of glowing likenesses of Mr. Gretzky.

It hardly needs to be said that there is no photographic record of the earliest phases, the origins, of the game. Curiously enough, it is another pictorial medium, painting – a 400-year-old oil painting, to be precise – that provides us with one of our more appreciable insights into hockey's beginnings. Growing up in Canada, we always believed hockey was a purely Canadian game. The Americans and Europeans played it, we knew, but we also knew they had borrowed it from us. Everybody said so. In introducing *The Hockey Book* in 1953, the late Bill Roche, a veteran hockey reporter, a man whose perspective on the game was as broad and perceptive as anyone's, wrote:

"Ice hockey is a game conceived and developed by Canadians. One might say it was born of necessity, for back in the 1870s the winters seemed long and dreary to the youth of our country. ...Happily, someone thought of using the abundant ice surfaces for a new game to be played on skates. The general pattern of the game was possibly England's field hockey."

Unknown to Mr. Roche, a version of hockey was being played in Europe at least as early as the 16th century, and perhaps much earlier. One of the few pieces of empirical evidence of this is a painting, 'The Hunters,' by Peter Breugel, a Flemish artist whose career spanned the middle decades of the 1500s. In the foreground of the painting are several hunters, trudging through snow, carrying their prey. In the distant valley below them, on a frozen river or canal, are a number of tiny figures who are discernibly carrying what could only be described as hockey sticks. Their various poses indicate strongly that they are skating (primitive wooden and metal skates, perhaps like those used by the fabled Hans Brinker, are known to have existed in Holland as early as the Middle Ages). Because of the scale of the painting, it is impossible to see a puck, though the presence of the sticks is powerful evidence that *something* is being shoved around on the ice.

One might argue that the game being played in the painting was not hockey as we know it. In the same vein, nor was the hockey played in 19th-century Canada hockey as we know it. One of the first Canadian games on record in the mid-1870s was a crowded fracas played in Montreal by 30 McGill University students, all of whom were on the ice at once. Some wore skates, some street shoes. The game was played with a ball.

By the time the first league was formed in 1885 in Kingston, Ontario, the game had evolved considerably, but was still being played under relatively primitive conditions. There were no goal nets, for instance – only small mounds of snow to indicate the width of the goal (the futurists of the day would occasionally ram small wooden goal-posts into the ice). There were no waist-high boards or bluelines, and the condition of the ice was often atrocious. In a championship game played in Rat Portage (now Kenora, Ontario) in the late 1800s, the puck was reported to have vanished into a wide crack in the ice, from which it could not be recovered.

The players of the day wore no specialized equipment other than their skates, which were not always entirely satisfactory pieces of gear. The skate blades, like those worn in Europe, were not riveted onto boots but were clamped onto street shoes in much the way that the inexpensive roller skates of the future would be attached to children's shoes. During the late 1940s, "Captain Jim" Sutherland, an early player with the Kingston Athletics, recalled a game in which the Athletics' goaltender was all but defeated by such skates:

"He was using his skates to block the ice-hugging shots. The impact would release the trigger-type fastener of the skate and the skate would fly off the goalie's boot and go sailing across the rink. The referee would then stop play, the skate would be replaced and the game would continue."

Until well into the 1890s, players, including goaltenders, wore no pads. They didn't have to; no one had yet figured out how to raise the puck, and errant sticks were not yet considered a sufficient threat to the shins. Then some bright innovator discovered the "backhand lift" shot, and within weeks goaltenders were showing up at rinks in borrowed cricket pads. Forwards, too, soon adopted the shin pad, a piece of equipment which, through the years, has probably known more variety of form than any other. During the 1930s, '40s and '50s, there were few young players in Canada who didn't know what it was to tuck a pair of Eaton's catalogues up under their jeans as a means of protecting their legs. Others used newspapers or chunks of corrugated cardboard. During the '60s and '70s, Bobby Hull (among other players) wrapped his lower legs in sheepskin,

**The Stanley Cup trophy** has undergone numerous alterations since 1893, when the Montreal AAA won the silver bowl shown at far right. Today's Stanley Cup is built around a duplicate of this original bowl. Each year, the names of every member of the winning team are engraved on the barrel of the Cup. The present Cup has room to accomodate these names until 1992, when the trophy will be 100 years old.

beneath his regular pads, to help absorb the constant thrashing he took from opposition players.

### Challenge for the Cup

It is sharp evidence of the popularity of the early game that, by 1893, leagues had been established across Canada, homogeneous rules had been laid down, and the governor general of the country, Lord Stanley, had donated the Stanley Cup, to be held by the top team in the Dominion. For the first 23 years of the Cup's existence, any team in Canada (and by 1916, any team anywhere) could challenge for it at any time during the hockey season. There were some unlikely claimants to the trophy. In 1905, the Ottawa Silver Seven, who held the Cup, were challenged by an irrepressible team of prospectors from Dawson City. It is a tale verging on myth how the Yukon team journeyed 4,000 miles by dogsled to Skagway, Alaska, took a boat to Vancouver and a train to Ottawa, where they were trashed 9-2 and 23-2 in successive games. Later that year, the Silver Seven were challenged by a team from Rat Portage, which they defeated with equal ease.

As furious as the early game must have appeared to its fans, it would likely seem unmercifully slow to observers today. For one thing, players spent the *entire game* on the ice (indeed, some did so right up into the 1930s). For a contemporary player to play even 60 percent of a game – say, 35 to 40 minutes – is considered a Promethean accomplishment, even with regular rests on the bench. Anyone who has ever played even 15 minutes

c. 1890

**Frederick Arthur,** Lord Stanley of Preston, Earl of Derby and Governor General of Canada, donated the trophy that bears his name in 1893. He stipulated that the Stanley Cup was a challenge trophy to be held from year to year by "the champion hockey club of the Dominion."

**Ottawa Silver Seven** Stanley Cup Champions — 1905. *Top row:* Harvey "Rat" Westwick, M. McGilton, Billy Gilmour, Frank McGee. *Bottom row:* Dave Finnie, Harvey Pulford, Alf Smith, Art Moore.

The Ottawa Silver Seven won three consecutive Stanley Cups from 1903 to 1905. This was a team of stars, with five of the seven players in this photograph elected to the Hockey Hall of Fame. Frank McGee was one of the first great scorers, netting 14 goals in one Stanley Cup game against Dawson City in 1905.

of spirited, non-stop hockey will understand, by the severe stress on the lungs and legs, that early players must have spent a fair portion of any game dawdling behind the play, attempting desperately to catch their wind. Moreover, the ice was crowded by nine-man teams, then seven-man teams, until 1911, when the six-man rule was introduced. As a further retardant, the early skates had flat blades, unlike today's "rockered" blades which add immeasurably to a skater's maneuverability. What's more, the ice was often snowy or soft, or badly chipped. There is a story, of somewhat dubious origin, that when the Ottawa Silver Seven traveled to Rat Portage for the first Stanley Cup series between the teams in 1903, the home team, not content to let the already faulty ice of their rink bring their renowned opponents into check, went to the rink the night before the first game and lightly salted the ice.

Perhaps the greatest contributor to the slow pace of early hockey was that it was an "onside" game, meaning that no forward passes were permitted and that the puck could only be advanced by the puck carrier. Those familiar with the game of rugger, which is also an onside game, will

c. 1935

**Foster Hewitt,** master broadcaster.

know that such games progress not by rapid acceleration of the sort that can be achieved by a forward pass but by the sheer cunning or brute force with which the lead man in the attack can move across the playing surface. Since, in hockey, the puck carrier's options were not great in number, checkers could easily gang up on him. In a tight spot, often the best he could do was to drop the puck to a teammate, give it up to the opposition or struggle on at the risk of being racked by a bodycheck.

Within a year of the founding of the NHL in 1917, hockey was liberated by a new rule permitting forward passing, at least in the neutral zone between bluelines. It would be 1929 before the forward pass would be allowed in all zones of the rink, but, nonetheless, the game sped up immeasurably with the 1918 ruling. Not surprisingly, the game also made great gains in popularity. By 1926, the original three-team NHL* (Toronto, Montreal and Ottawa) had increased to 10 teams, including six in the United States.

*There had initially been four teams in the NHL, but the Montreal Wanderers were forced to withdraw when their arena burnt down after six games of the first schedule.

### Effective ambassador

But pro hockey's popularity did not increase entirely on the considerable merits of the game. It had, and still has, salesmen, promoters, ambassadors: the Patricks, Norrises, Selkes, Smythes; Gordie Howe, Bobby Hull, Bobby Orr, Guy Lafleur; now Wayne Gretzky. In the overall history of the sport, however, no one has served as a more effective ambassador than a round-faced, shrill-voiced broadcaster named Foster Hewitt. Former NHL coach and manager Punch Imlach once said, "He did more for hockey than any man alive." Hewitt not only popularized the early NHL, but simultaneously made a legendary figure of himself through his Saturday night broadcasts from Maple Leaf Gardens in Toronto.

Late in August of 1957, or was it '58?, I traveled to Toronto with my parents to visit the Canadian National Exhibition. We stayed at the home of relatives, and on the first day of the visit, at the first opportunity, I stole into the master bedroom, took out the Toronto phone book and looked up the number of an ever-so-familiar name – F. Hewitt. I quietly dialed the number, and within a ring or two, the receiver at the other end was lifted. Why I should have been surprised I don't know – it was his number after all (perhaps I had expected an intermediary of some sort) – but there on the wire, clear as a Saturday night broadcast, was his voice, *the* voice, whose high-pitched cadence had excited and deflated me on so many Saturday nights.

I politely said hello and told Mr. Hewitt who I was. Not really having anything else to say, but sensing by his slowness to respond that the conversation wasn't going to go very far, I quickly told him that I had simply phoned to say I always listened to his broadcasts.

"Well, I'm glad to hear that," he said.

I then asked him who his favorite players were. There was a pause, and he said warmly, "I like them all," and the conversation was over.

What was significant was not, of course, our meager exchange of words but that I, a young hockey fanatic, considered Foster Hewitt, not Frank Mahovlich or Tim Horton, no, that I considered a middle-aged broadcaster, hardly the model of a sports hero, my foremost link with NHL hockey. Millions of others felt exactly the same way.

Hewitt's first broadcast was made from Toronto's Mutual Street Arena in March 1923 when, as a young reporter for the *Toronto Star*, he was asked to deliver a play-by-play report of a game between a Toronto Parkdale team and one from Kitchener. He was soon broadcasting professional games, and when Maple Leaf Gardens opened for business in 1931, he was there in his gondola to broadcast the inaugural game between the Black Hawks and the Maple Leafs.

In his autobiography, the late Conn Smythe, the founder of the Maple Leafs, recalled that when he built the Gardens, he told Hewitt to tell the designers exactly where his broadcast booth should be. "Foster went to a tall building," wrote Smythe, "and walked from floor to floor, looking at the people on the street below until he decided that the fifth-floor height, fifty-six feet, was best – and that's the height at which his gondola was built."

When Hewitt died in April 1985 no one paid him more poetic tribute than did Trent Frayne of Toronto's *Globe and Mail*:

"Those of us who grew up on the prairies listening to his voice will never forget him coming over the airways and greeting us. 'Hello Canada and hockey fans in the United States and Newfoundland,' he'd say. 'The score at the end of the first period is...' And then he'd tell us, the millions of us spread right across the country, brought together in living rooms and kitchens and bathtubs and cars and on lonely dark farms and in small snow-packed towns and in big brightly lit cities from one ocean to the other, all of us in our mind's eye watching the matchless giants on the ice below."

### Lifted from your seat

In the early years of Hewitt's broadcasts, the greatest of those matchless giants were players such as King Clancy, Charlie Conacher and Joe Primeau of the Leafs, Eddie Shore of the Bruins, Frank Boucher of the Rangers and, perhaps the most matchless of them all, Howie Morenz of the Montreal Canadiens. Morenz was the game's first real superstar, appealing to the fans in a way that no other player had ever done. Montreal journalist Andy O'Brien, who covered the Canadiens during Morenz's career, once compared him to a compact version of Bobby Hull.

"He would challenge the opposing defenses by dazzling dash and deception," said O'Brien. "You didn't have to know anything about hockey

**The first** New York Americans pose for their inaugural team photograph outside Madison Square Garden in October 1925. That season the Amerks won 12 of 36 games and finished fifth out of seven teams in the NHL.

1925

**Howie Morenz** played with New York Rangers for part of the 1936-'37 season. His stardom came in Montreal.

to be lifted from your seat by Morenz – just as you didn't have to know anything about baseball to be thrilled by a towering home run by Babe Ruth." Morenz was, in fact, sometimes referred to as the Babe Ruth of hockey. When he died in 1937 of complications from a severe hockey injury, 14,000 bemused and silent fans crowded the Montreal Forum for his funeral. Another 200,000 are said to have jammed the streets to watch his cortege roll past on the way to Mount Royal cemetery.

Morenz, whose career in the NHL began in 1923 and spanned 14 years, was a major force, perhaps *the* major force, in convincing American promoters that hockey was not merely a sport for the frigid cities of the north, but a big-league attraction for the American metropolis. It was only a year after Morenz joined the Canadiens in 1924 that the NHL crossed the American border for the first time to Boston. But then, as now, the New York area was seen by the league as its most lucrative market, and the following year, New York promoter Tex Rickard, having seen Morenz perform, was easily persuaded to take control of the insurgent Hamilton Tigers, who that season had undertaken the league's first labor walk-out, and move them to New York, where they became the New York Americans.

Until then, Madison Square Garden, where the team was to play, had not even had ice-making equipment. Rickard, a legendary entrepreneur who a year earlier had built the Boston Garden, introduced his new team to New York with a lavish display of press flack and showmanship. For the opening game, which was also part of the formal opening of the Garden, Rickard persuaded league president Frank Calder to book Morenz and the Canadiens into town. Unlike today's schedule, which begins early in October, that year's season began on December 15, and Rickard was able to wheedle the crust of New York's social elite into attending the initial game. The guest list included such names as Carnegie, Rothschild, Crowningshield, Barnum, Ringling and Mayor Jimmy Walker. A front page article in the *New York Times* the next day reported:

"A lot of water will flow under the Brooklyn Bridge before New York witnesses a sporting carnival with so much fuss and ostentation as that which attended the introduction of pro hockey in Gotham.... The lobby looked like the foyer of the opera: furs, jewels, flashes of cerise, Nile greens...

The Canadiens paraded around the ice behind the Governor General's Foot Guards band (ablaze in red coats and gold braid). The Americans skated behind the military band from West Point (with white-lined capes thrown back over their shoulders."

But in spite of the fanfare and heavy partisan support, the home team lost the game 3-1, as it would lose so many more over the 16 years of its desultory existence. But the fans and newsmen were, nonetheless, impressed by the initial contest. The *Times* reporter described the play as "fast and furious," the checking as "vigorously rough." Hockey, he announced confidently, was "sure to gain popularity."

That same year, 1925, the Pittsburgh Pirates, a team that lasted only five years, also joined the NHL. The following year, the league made its biggest expansion prior to 1967, as three more American teams materialized: The Chicago Black Hawks, the New York Rangers and the Detroit Cougars, a predecessor of the Red Wings.

## Five-star whoppers

If Howie Morenz was the premier attraction of the day, he had a close competitor in the late Eddie Shore. Nicknamed "the Edmonton Express," Shore joined the new Boston Bruin franchise during the 1926 season. He is said to have played his position on defense in a style similar to that of a future Boston star, Bobby Orr, making frequent lightning rushes on the opposition's goal. What set Shore apart from other skaters, however, was not only his technical skill but what one journalist referred to as "his absurd fearlessness and dedication." There are perhaps a hundred eminently retellable Eddie Shore stories (many of them five-star whoppers), but the one that most roundly embodies the man's attitude to the game is that of his harrowing blizzard drive from Boston to Montreal in January 1929.

The story goes this way: Eddie was trying to get to a game in Montreal, but on the way to the train his cab got stalled in a blizzard. Having missed the train, he telephoned an affluent friend and talked him into lending him a car and a chauffeur. After a few hours of driving through heavy snow in the treacherous mountains of New England, the windshield wipers broke and visibility was cut to zero. The chauffeur refused to go on, so Shore grabbed the wheel, flipped open the old-style windshield and drove on with the snow and wind swirling around his head. Four times he skidded off the road and each time managed to get the car out of the ditch, once with the help of a farmer's team of horses. After driving 14 hours without stopping, he arrived shortly before game time, suffering not only profound exhaustion but a severe case of frostbite. Nevertheless, he insisted on playing, and, except for a two-minute penalty, was on the ice for the entire game.

Boston won 1-0, with Eddie Shore scoring the game's only goal.

Shore's obsessive personality got him into numerous fights, one of which led, near tragically, to the staging of the first NHL all-star game. It is frequently recalled how, on December 12, 1933, at the Boston Garden, Shore, in a moment of ferocity against the opposing Maple Leafs, skated up quickly on Leaf left wing Ace Bailey and bodychecked him from behind. Bailey's head struck the ice, and within hours he was in a Boston hospital undergoing brain surgery to relieve the pressure of a massive concussion. For days, newspaper and radio reports followed his dramatic battle for survival.

Bailey, who had been a player of skill and refinement, never returned to hockey, and for some time Eddie Shore was held in powerful contempt by NHL fans. But those feelings were mollified on St. Valentine's night in 1934, when a team of NHL all-stars, the first ever chosen, came to Maple Leaf Gardens to play the Leafs in a benefit game for Bailey. Before the opening face-off, Bailey walked cautiously to center ice, wearing dark glasses and a knee-length overcoat. As he reached the face-off circle, Shore, who had asked to be included in the all-star lineup, skated out from where his teammates were stationed along the blueline and extended his hand to Bailey, who immediately accepted the gesture of reconciliation. A famous photo, probably snapped just after the handshake at center ice, shows the two men at the boards restaging their meeting. Bailey, who looks more like a young business executive than a recent victim of the NHL trenches, is smiling warmly and looking directly, albeit through dark glasses, into Shore's eyes. Shore's smile, though present, is tentative and directed not at Bailey but down at the ice or to the boards in the lower distance.

## Fittest and toughest

To bastardize the term somewhat, pro hockey was then, and is now, a game of survival of the fittest – or, in some cases, survival of the toughest. It is a game of astonishing perseverance. Injuries, for instance, that, should they befall the average human being, would impinge on his thoughts and

**Irvin "Ace" Bailey,** left, greets Eddie Shore at the first meeting between the two men since Shore's blindside bodycheck ended Bailey's hockey career. Bailey had played with Toronto since 1927, winning the NHL's goal and point-scoring championships in 1929. That year he recorded 32 goals and 10 assists in 44 games.

1934

**Defenseman Bob Baun** played the sixth and seventh games of the 1964 Stanley Cup Final on a broken leg.

1964

1952

**"Rocket Richard's greatest goal** had to have been the one he scored on Sugar Jim Henry in the seventh game of the 1952 semi-finals. He had been knocked out, but came back to score the winner late in the game. He carried the puck from his own end, swept around the left defense and broke in on goal to score. The Bruins had a defenseman named Gus Kyle who used to give the Rocket all kinds of trouble, but he wasn't dressed for the last couple of games of the series. Kyle played the left side, so we always wondered if the Rocket would have been able to break in if he had been on the ice at that time." — *Dick Irvin*

Henry and the Rocket meet at the game's end, above.

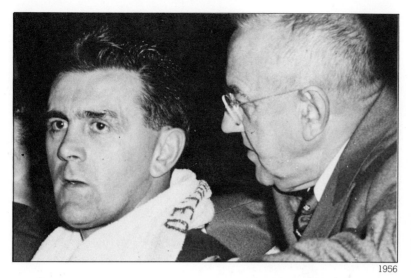

**Even on the bench,** Richard's gaze penetrates. At right is managing director Frank Selke, Sr.

1956

mobility for days, if not weeks, are treated only as seriously as the number of games, or minutes of games, that will be missed on their account.

During the 1980 playoffs, in a game against the Minnesota North Stars, Montreal's Rejean Houle suffered a stupefying blow to the mouth that knocked out several teeth and severely lacerated his gums. Taking just enough time to have his wounds stitched, he returned to the game, finished it with a flourish, *and* conducted an enthusiastic television interview.

Another instance of near-maniacal fortitude was Toronto defenseman Bob Baun's insistence on playing the last game of the 1964 Stanley Cup final while liberally pumped up with pain killer to cover the agony of a broken leg suffered in the previous game. Players regularly play with fractured jaws, broken noses, plate-sized bruises and multi-stitch cuts. As Gordie Howe said, "It's a man's game."

### The Rocket's red glare

Perhaps the most legendary feat of perseverance occurred at the Montreal Forum during the seventh game of the 1952 semi-finals between the Canadiens and Boston Bruins. During the second period, Rocket Richard was bodychecked fiercely by Leo Labine, causing him to fall headfirst into defenseman Bill Quackenbush's knee. For several minutes the Rocket lay on the ice, and there was fear that his neck had been broken. He was eventually carried to the Forum clinic, where a deep gash in his forehead was stitched shut. During the third period, not fully conscious, he insisted on returning to the Canadiens' bench, where he sat gazing dimly at the clock. When Elmer Lach told him there were four minutes to go in the game, which was tied 1-1, he turned to coach Dick Irvin and told him he was ready. Andy O'Brien describes what followed:

"Rocket picked up a pass from Canadien defenseman Butch Bouchard beside his own net and ducked by a forechecker, veering toward center ice. In four strides he eluded the other winger who had cut in sharply. He veered right, away from the Boston center's reaching poke-check.

Over the Boston blueline, defenseman Bob Armstrong and Quackenbush were skating backwards. Richard tried to circle Quackenbush, but the cagey veteran rode him towards the boards. Richard was still in high gear, however; shoving Quackenbush aside with his left arm, he switched in sharply toward the Boston goalmouth. Unable to wait, Armstrong surged forward. Richard button-hooked around him and swooped in on the frantic goalie, Sugar Jim Henry, who was squinting through a face that had suffered a broken nose and two black eyes earlier in the game.

There was a flurry of sticks, Henry dove, Richard pulled the puck aside and blasted the netting."

There is a historic photo of the Rocket shaking hands with Sugar Jim following the game. The great Montreal shooter is staring catatonically at the smaller goalie, his forehead bandaged, blood still streaming over his face. Sugar Jim is half bowed, as if to say, "You win, Mr. Richard, you win."

After the game, team president Senator Donat Raymond entered the Canadiens' dressing room to congratulate his star. As he took Richard's hand, the Rocket began to sob, then broke into explosive convulsions that were only calmed when the team doctor injected Richard with a sedative. In the course of the Rocket's long rush up the ice, there had been a number of opportunities to pass the puck; and it was not understood until later that he had kept control only because his vision had been too blurry to pick out a teammate to whom he could pass.

The Rocket, who played in the NHL from 1942 to 1960, is thought by many to be the most spirited professional that the game has ever known. In an era in which scoring 20 goals in a season was considered a mark of excellence, the Rocket several times scored more than twice that many and, once, during the 1944-'45 season, scored 50 goals in 50 games, a record that stood until 1982.

But it wasn't just the *number* of goals that Richard scored; it was the way he scored them. Hall of Fame goaltender Frank Brimsek once said, "He could shoot from any angle. You could play him for a shot to the upper corner and the Rocket would wheel around and fire a backhander to the near, lower part of the net." Another Hall of Famer, goaltender Glenn Hall, said of Richard, "When he skated in on net, his eyes would shine like a pair of searchlights. It was awesome to see him coming at you."

It was indeed the Rocket's eyes that signaled the spirit within. Even in mere publicity photos his eyes burned with an animal passion – the Rocket's Red Glare, it has been called – that seemed to verge on dementia. During the early 1950s, novelist William Faulkner, on a special assignment for *Sports Illustrated* magazine, went to Madison Square Garden to watch a game between the New York Rangers and the Canadiens. A short time later, he wrote that one player, Richard, had stood out beyond the others with a "passionate, glittering, fatal, alien quality of snakes."

1961

**Gordie Howe, with his tremendous strength,** was called "Power" by his teammates. Toronto goalie Johnny Bower was known as "The Snake" for his ability to poke-check opposing players with his big goal stick.

Though they faced each other in many big games, the two were great friends. "Johnny Bower was from Prince Albert and Gordie Howe from Floral — both in Saskatchewan. I recall reading of the incident in a playoff game when Bower fell in the crease and Howe was there to pick up the loose puck. In the newspapers, Bower said that instead of shooting, Howe shouted, 'Look out, Johnny!'" — *Ken Dryden*

Commenting on the potency of the Rocket's personality, Frank Selke, Sr., former managing director of the Canadiens, once said that even when the Rocket wasn't playing, the sheer force of his personality could lift the team. "All he had to do was to be in the dressing room or on the bench. Nobody dared clown around when he was in there. He came to win, and the others caught the spirit from him. No one could take liberties with our team when he was there, and opposing players knew it."

### Howe's power

Richard is often compared to the game's other Titan of the era, Gordie Howe. In fact, at one time, a series of quasi-scientific tests were conducted to compare the two players' skills. But whether one of them was superior to the other is finally a question of marginal significance. Each in his way contributed mightily – mythically – to the game and its fans.

A curious thing about Howe was that he didn't always *seem* to be do-ing that much on the ice. At times he appeared downright leisurely; his

1952

**Before his great career** began in Montreal, Jean Beliveau was the world's best-known "amateur" hockey player when he played with the Quebec Aces in 1952 and 1953.

stride was measured, his checking controlled, his shot a powerful but unexaggerated flick of the wrists. He relied not on dash but on remarkable strength and subtlety and could often accomplish in one motion, or a half-motion, what other players took two or three moves to achieve. If, for instance, he was being checked from the right side (his shooting side), instead of shifting frantically, or whirling, or powering to a stop, he would often simply switch his stick to the other side of his body, change hands on it, and drill the puck ambidextrously from the left.

Another curious thing about Howe was that, in spite of the apparent modesty of his style, he was more often than not at the focal point of the play: making a pass, setting up a shot, taking a shot – and always with that deadly efficiency and strength. Given the tough, defensive standards under which he played in his prime, Howe's 1,071 career goals are an almost unaccountable record for major-league hockey – the equivalent of 21 fifty-goal seasons (Wayne Gretzky or Mike Bossy will surely have to score 2,000 goals to approximate Howe's total). Howe's 34-year career – nearly twice as long as the Rocket's, nearly three times as long as Bobby

Orr's – is an unprecedented record for *any* major-league sport. Six times he won the NHL scoring title, six times the most-valuable-player award. He played in 22 all-star games. Shortly before he retired in 1980 at the age of 52, he said, "I don't really know why I go on. It's not the money, and I've certainly had my share of glory. The thing is, this isn't a job to me. It's a way of life, and nobody teaches you how to give it up."

### Stacked with talent

It is hardly surprising that the Canadiens and Red Wings of the late 1940s and '50s, years in which Howe and Richard were in their dominance, were hockey's preeminent teams. Beginning with the 1948-'49 season, the Red Wings had seven successive first-place finishes. They had another in 1956-'57, while the Canadiens finished first every other year until 1960. The two teams – the Wings of the early '50s, the Canadiens of the late '50s – are thought by many to have been the greatest hockey teams ever assembled. Though such assessments are far from empirical (hockey fans have an inordinate penchant for speculation), there is certainly ample evidence for the notion. Both teams were stacked with what in later years would be called "franchise" players. In addition to the Rocket, Montreal had Jean Beliveau, Doug Harvey, Bernie Geoffrion, Dickie Moore, Tom Johnson, Henri Richard, and defensive specialist Claude Provost (one of few checkers ever to effectively restrict Bobby Hull). The talented and inventive Jacques Plante played goal. In addition to Howe, the Red Wings' lineup included Alex Delvecchio, Ted Lindsay, Sid Abel, Red Kelly, Marcel Pronovost and the brilliant but ill-fated Terry Sawchuk in goal. Any talented assemblage of players is inclined to increase the stature of its coach, but there is little doubt that Toe Blake of the Canadiens and Tommy Ivan and Jimmy Skinner of the Wings also contributed substantially to the strength and spirit of those great teams.

1949

**Toe Blake** coached eight Stanley Cup winning teams with Montreal from 1955 to 1968.

### Firepower and defense

A later version of the Canadiens, the four-time Stanley Cup winners of the mid- to late '70s, would certainly have given the Habs of the '50s a potent, if hypothetical, challenge. Like their forebears, the Habs of the '70s were a pretty well seamless cohesion of firepower and defense. The players' names alone are redolent of the totality with which they dominated the league during their championship seasons: Guy Lafleur, Larry Robinson, Serge Savard, Guy Lapointe, Yvan Cournoyer, Steve Shutt, Jacques Lemaire, Pete Mahovlich, Ken Dryden. To neutralize other teams' shooters, coach Scotty Bowman could deploy Doug Jarvis and Bob Gainey, or Rejean Houle, or Jimmy Roberts, all of whom were among the league's ranking defensive forwards. During the 1976-'77 season, the team lost only eight of 80 games, and established an all-time record for team points.

### The Flower

But none of it would have been possible without the poetic talents of Guy Lafleur, the charmed inheritor of the great Canadien line of succession: Morenz... Richard... Beliveau. Like Jean Beliveau, Lafleur had a storied pre-NHL career in Quebec City. As a Junior there, he filled the hometown Colisée with worshippers. On the road, he drew capacity crowds in Cornwall, Trois Rivières, Drummondville, Sherbrooke, Verdun. If the Remparts were in town, which is to say if Lafleur were in town, it was all but axiomatic that the local rink would be packed.

At the height of his career Lafleur played with an almost preternatural combination of skills and spirit. There were nights when his physical and motivational edge was practically indefensible to opposition players. However, unlike some of the game's masters – Howe, Hull, Beliveau, Orr – Lafleur was not an "effortless" player. His skating, though mercurial in speed, often seemed choppy, his moves not entirely efficient; he would swerve, dodge, whirl, skate wildly into a corner; he would crash on the brakes at an unexpected moment – always at top energy, and always with an implied glee at what he was doing to frustrate his opponents.

If a player could be said to have a career-crowning game, Lafleur's came on May 11, 1979, in the seventh game of the Stanley Cup semi-finals against the Boston Bruins. The series had been gladiatorially tough, and with 14 minutes to go in the deciding contest, the Canadiens were down 3-1 and seemed doomed by the sensational goaltending of Gilles Gilbert. But from the beginning of the third period, Lafleur had been pressing relentlessly, and just past the six-minute point he fed Mark Napier, who wristed a shot past Gilbert, putting the Canadiens within a goal of the Bruins.

Two minutes later it was again Lafleur, this time setting up Guy Lapointe, who fired a screen shot past the Bruin goalie. But with less than four minutes left, Rick Middleton of the Bruins took a pass from Jean Ratelle, skated from behind the Canadiens' goal and put a shot off Ken Dryden's glove into the corner of the net. The Forum, which had been rabid with excitement, was silenced. "I thought it was over," said Coach Scotty Bowman. "It gets that late in a game, it looked like the goalie was going to beat us."

With one minute, 14 seconds left in regulation time, however, Lafleur, seemingly determined that the Habs should not be beaten, powered down the right wing into the Bruins' end of the rink, and from along the boards some 40 feet from the net, cranked a shot that howled by Gilbert and again tied the game. The shot came from such a distance and with such force – and into such a narrow opening in the net – that Bruin coach Don Cherry would later say, "Lafleur, and only Lafleur, could have scored on that shot."

The Canadiens won the game in overtime and proceeded to the final in which they defeated the New York Rangers for the Stanley Cup.

### Gretzky's glitter

Seldom has a team achieved greatness, even briefly, without at least one glittering, dominating player – a player on the order of Richard or Howe or Lafleur. The great Bruin teams of the late '60s and early '70s had Bobby Orr; the Flyers of a few years later had Bobby Clarke; the Black Hawks of 1960-'61 had Bobby Hull. Today's Edmonton Oilers have Wayne Gretzky, arguably the most skillful player in the history of the game. Though certain players – Gordie Howe or Bryan Trottier, for instance – have exhibited superior all-around skills, no one has ever shown Gretzky's genius for combining the arts of passing, puckhandling, skating and scoring – and timing. Gretzky has an uncanny ability to release a pass at exactly the right moment; to hold back a shot until an opposition defenseman or goalie is precisely where Gretzky wants him; to anticipate precisely what an opposition player will do with the puck. Gordie Howe said of Gretzky, "Wayne's the only guy who plays 70 percent of the game from the neck up." Said Henri Richard, "He has the greatest moves I've ever seen."

1977

**"After Guy Lafleur's third year** in the NHL, the Canadiens considered trading him. Sam Pollack called Scotty Bowman and Claude Ruel into his office and said, 'What do you think?' Bowman and Ruel said that they still thought he was going to be fine, so the Canadiens signed him to a long-term contract.

Then in his fourth season, Lafleur took off his helmet. Montreal played its first league game against the New York Islanders, and right from the first face-off, he was a huge presence on the ice. That was his first fifty-goal year."
— *Dick Irvin*

In 1982, Gretzky smashed through hockey's 50 goal/50 game barrier with a ferocity, scoring 50 goals in 39 games and 92 goals for the season. Even by today's high-scoring standards, the 39-game record seems all but unapproachable – unless, of course, approached by Gretzky himself.

### The Orr style

Other than Lafleur, the only player of the past 15 years whose skating, passing and puckhandling were within hailing distance of Gretzky's is Bobby Orr, whose only definable weaknesses were his notoriously vulnerable knees. When Orr joined the Bruins in 1966, they were the serfs of the league, having finished out of the playoffs for the past seven years. By 1970 they had won the Stanley Cup.

Unlike his peers, if he could be said to have had peers, Orr's true genius was not so much stopping goals as creating them. Which was far from a defensive drawback. There is an archaic hockey adage that the best defense is a good offense. When Orr had the puck, as he frequently did, playing up to 40 minutes a game, the opposition, by definition, did not have the puck. In 1970, the Bruins' star became the first defenseman to win the league scoring championship with 33 goals and 87 assists for a total of 120 points. A season later, he upped this total to 139.

It was Orr who demonstrated the importance of mobility and skating

**"I remember being in front** of the Boston net when I got whacked on the side of the head by Bobby Orr's stick as he was trying to move me out of the way. I looked up and saw who hit me, and as he made one of his accurate passes from behind the net, I drilled him. We both fell to the ice and the whistle blew. The Boston players automatically came to his aid and he said, 'Relax guys, I deserved it.' He came into the NHL with the talent and the head of a veteran."
— *Gordie Howe*

1966

1964

**Bobby Hull's strength and speed** forced opposing coaches to shadow him with their top checkers.

prowess for modern NHL defensemen. He ended the long-held notion that strong skaters usually played on the forward line, while weaker ones lined up at defense. Many observers of hockey feel that this change, inspired by Bobby Orr, distinguishes today's hockey.

Orr's impact cannot be overestimated. His agent, Alan Eagleson, said, "Bobby's the only player capable of filling every rink in the NHL" – a claim which, over the years, would prove itself thoroughly. Orr's coach, Harry Sinden, once said, "Howe could do everything, but not at top speed. Hull went at top speed but couldn't do everything. Orr could do everything *and* do it at top speed."

## The Golden Jet

If, as Sinden said, Bobby Hull couldn't do everything, he could certainly do most of the things that make hockey the dramatic attraction it is. He could outskate almost everybody in the league during the 1960s. He could outmuscle them. He could outscore them handily. Off the ice, he could outsmile them, and for nearly two decades was the most personable and gregarious of hockey's superstars. In 1966, he became the first player to surpass Rocket Richard's longstanding single-season record of 50 goals.

The two attributes that most characterized Hull's game were his magnificent skating and his equally magnificent shot. His signature move, the one for which his fans best remember him, was to accelerate across the blueline on the left wing (either with the puck or to receive a pass), to raise his stick to an exaggerated height and pound an obliterative slapshot at the net. When he wound up to shoot, a momentary paralysis would grip the crowd – and undoubtedly the opposition goaltender. Hull's shots were said to travel at speeds of up to 120 miles per hour. In the words of goaltender Les Binkley, "When the puck left his stick, it looked like a pea. Then as it picked up speed it looked smaller and smaller. Then you didn't see it anymore."

Although the slapshot had been used by a number of players in the 1960s – notably Boom-Boom Geoffrion and Andy Bathgate – it was Hull who popularized it on a grand scale, who sent hundreds of thousands of school boys scurrying to their neighborhood rinks – or their driveways or basements – to practice the sometimes unpredictable shot. With Stan Mikita, Hull also popularized the curved stick blade, another significant contributor to the unpredictability of a fired puck.

When Hull left the Black Hawks in 1972 and signed with the Winnipeg Jets of the then-fragile World Hockey Association, he gave instant cachet not only to the Jets but to the entire league. Had he not lent his formidable presence to the new league, whose solvency quotient at the time was approximately that of distilled water on marble, there would quite likely have been no league after a season or two; and the Winnipeg Jets, Edmonton Oilers, Quebec Nordiques and Hartford Whalers would almost certainly not be part of the NHL today.

### Rink-rat in the big time

Among modern greats, Bobby Clarke came as close as anyone to being Bobby Hull's antithesis. Like Hull, Clarke could, at his peak, dominate almost any game in which he played. Unlike Hull, his natural skills were not great. They were, in fact, closer to the skills of a rink-rat than those of a modern superstar. He had neither great speed nor strength (he is a diabetic). Nor did he have exceptional size or an outstanding shot. Perhaps his greatest technical skill was an ability to win face-offs, an acquired, not a natural talent. What Clarke did have, and what inspired the Philadelphia Flyers in their Stanley Cup years, was an incalculable will – an inner force, which not only represented the spirit of the team but actually *was* the spirit of the team. Like the Rocket, Clarke could guide the play of his teammates, imbue them with energy, even when he was not on the ice.

Anyone who witnessed the 1977 quarter-finals between the Flyers and the Toronto Maple Leafs was certainly apprised of the effect of Clarke's will to win. With the Flyers down two goals in the fourth game and less than two minutes to play, and with the Leafs threatening to take a 3-1 lead in games, Clarke came onto the ice with an intractable, almost demonically determined expression on his face. He was squinting, as usual, and his toothless mouth was locked in a ferocious grimace. It was as if he had said to himself not merely we *must* score, but we *will* score, we are *going* to score, we are going to score *now*. Within half a minute, by brute force of will, he had engineered the goals that tied the game, and the Flyers went on to win in overtime.

### Tribal strong-man

Unlike the Flyers, Canadiens, Red Wings or Bruins, the great Maple Leaf teams of the 1960s – and indeed of the '40s – achieved their success without the guidance of a single, dominating player. Conn Smythe once described Red Horner (a pugnacious, reliable, but generally unspectacular defenseman) as the epitome of the Leaf teams of the 1930s and '40s. Bob Pulford, another effective but unremarkable player, was often said to epitomize the Leafs of the '60s. As Pulford goes, the saying was, so go the Maple Leafs.

Certain Leafs of the 1960s might well have shone more lustrously under different guidance. But Punch Imlach, their coach and general manager in Toronto, was at the time the closest thing the NHL had to a tribal strong-man. With Punch, the team was everything, individual glitter a weakness, a flaw in the system. Even Bert Olmstead, an archetypal team player who virtually lived in the corners working for the glory of others, is said to have complained about the Imlach school of conformity. Carl

1964         1959

**When Punch Imlach,** left, coached the Maple Leafs, the team won four Cups. Imlach was particularly tough on his star player, Frank Mahovlich, right.

Brewer, one of the most talented defensemen ever to play for the Leafs, went so far as to leave the team on account of the coach.

But the most celebrated Imlach antagonist was undoubtedly Frank Mahovlich who, from the moment Imlach joined the Leafs in 1958 to the moment Frank departed from them in 1967, was at odds with his boss. Shortly after Mahovlich became a Leaf in 1957, he was christened "The Big M" – "M" for Moses, said King Clancy; and it was indeed understood that Frank would lead the Leafs into Canaan. He was powerful, he could skate; he could shoot bullets. As he once said of himself, "There were times it seemed I could just bull my way through the opposition.... Some nights, no matter who they put on me, I knew I could handle it." Mahovlich's winning of the Calder trophy as rookie of the year in 1957-'58 (he nosed out Bobby Hull) seemed to justify the expectations for him.

But in spite of his prodigious gifts, Mahovlich truly met his potential in only one year of 10 with the Maple Leafs – the 1960-'61 season, when he scored 48 goals. The following year he slid to 33, then 36, then 26 and 23. Meanwhile, Imlach needled him constantly – invariably referring to him as "Mahalavitch," telling the press that the Leafs would be fine if "Mahalavitch" would live up to expectations (this, in spite of Mahovlich's leading the Leafs in scoring every year from 1960 to 1966).

By the mid-'60s Frank had been pushed too far. Twice he suffered nervous breakdowns, and in 1967, after the Leafs' last Cup victory, he was traded to the Detroit Red Wings. A few years later he was again traded, this time to the Montreal Canadiens. It is perhaps irony, perhaps coincidence, maybe absolutely predictable, that having left the Leafs, Mahovlich played the best hockey of his career, and the Leafs, who had won four Stanley Cups with Frank in the lineup, have not won in the nearly 20 years since.

All of which is not to suggest that the Leaf teams of the '60s were not superb hockey teams. With their stolid emphasis on checking and "experience" (at one time they had two players more than 40 years old), they simply weren't everybody's idea of three-ring showmanship. When they last won the Stanley Cup in 1967, the players on the ice at the final buzzer of the last game – Pulford, Armstrong, Kelly, Horton, Stanley, Sawchuk – were, on average, nearly 38 years of age.

Though light years from the Leafs in most aspects, the championship Islanders of 1979 to 1983 were, of all the great teams of the modern era, most closely linked to the Toronto teams of the '60s – not, mind you, in their age or individual talents, but in their emphatic teamwork and balance – and their ability to win without a single, dominating player, such as Orr, Lafleur or Gretzky. Coach Al Arbour, like Imlach in strategy if not temperament, resolutely shaped the talents of players such as Bryan Trottier, Mike Bossy and Denis Potvin to the greater good of the team. It may be more than coincidence that Arbour, who coached the Islanders to four Stanley Cup victories, was a Leaf defenseman, a two-time Cup winner, under none other than Punch Imlach.

## Superior goaltending

It is practically a given of hockey that teams do not win championships without superior goaltending. Name the Cup winners of the past 40 years and you invariably find them staffed with the leading goalies of the day: Jacques Plante, Glenn Hall, Johnny Bower, Terry Sawchuk, Bernie Parent, Ken Dryden, Billy Smith.

But champions or not, goaltenders own a special status, a singular level of admiration, among hockey players. For it is they, more than any others, who manifest the primitive mystique of the game. They are the poets, the restless spirits, the eccentrics of hockey. Their equipment alone says volumes about the uniqueness of their work – layer upon layer of leather, cotton wadding, plastic and fiberglass. The armored knights of the Middle Ages were no better protected, perhaps not nearly as well.

Among the more telling representations of the goaltender's sensibilities are the vibrantly painted, molded masks popular with goalies of the 1970s. (Today most goaltenders wear wire masks.) A collection of the masks hangs in the Hockey Hall of Fame in Toronto, looking more like Transylvanian tribal-wear or primitive African death costuming than NHL hockey equipment. Gilles Gratton, who played during the mid-1970s with the St. Louis Blues and the New York Rangers, wore the image of a howling, ghoulish-looking tiger on his mask. John Garrett went into battle as a masked assassin, while Gary Bromley affected the countenance of a morbid cartoon skeleton.

It is apparent even to those who know little about hockey that the goaltender (in spite of his equipment) is in grave danger every time a forward or defenseman winds up for a shot. To watch game films from the 1950s and to see, for instance, a maskless Terry Sawchuk squatting in readiness in his crease, thrusting out his unprotected face to better see the puck screaming toward him through a maze of players – to see him there, apparently heedless of the risk to his life, is positively daunting to the contemporary viewer. Even in the present era of masked goaltenders, there can be few fans who have not cringed to see a goaltender felled by a shot to his unprotected throat or neck.

For the purposes of a photo, a physiotherapist once inked in every suture scar on Terry Sawchuk's face. The recreated tracks so thoroughly covered the goaltender's visage that the effect was closer to that of a knitted balaclava than an assemblage of facial features. Some years later, Gerry Cheevers gained the same effect by painting onto his mask the scars that *would* have been, had he not been wearing facial protection.

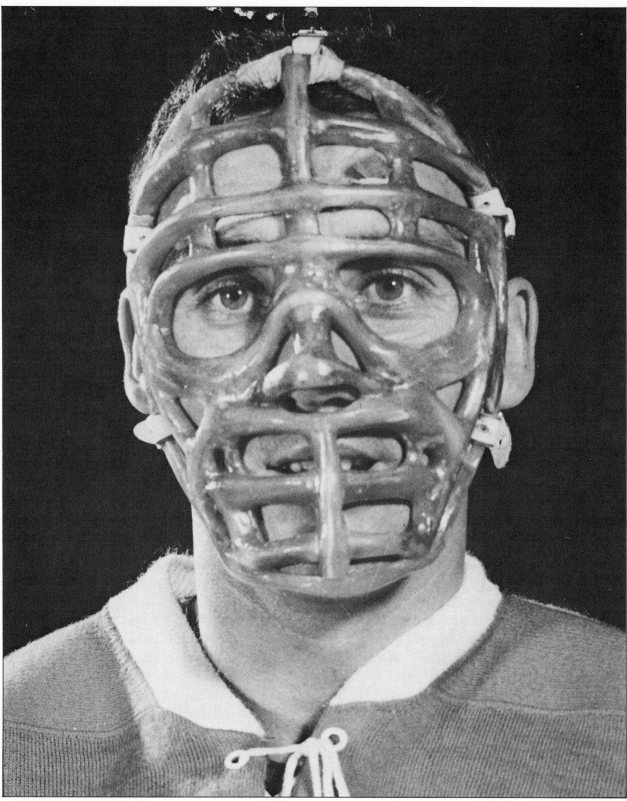

1960

1965

**Jacques Plante,** left, changed goaltending by developing the protective facemask. Plante was also the first goaltender to leave his crease to control the puck, aiding his team's defense.

Glenn Hall, right, set a record for durability in goal, appearing in 502 consecutive games for the Red Wings and the Black Hawks from 1956 to 1963.

Plante and Hall later became teammates and shared the Vezina Trophy as top goaltenders in the NHL with the St. Louis Blues in 1969.

## Goaltender's nerves

The inherent dangers of the goaltender's art are borne better by some than others. Throughout his career, Terry Sawchuk suffered from intense nervous disorders, at one point retiring prematurely (he returned to hockey the next season), claiming that his nerves were "completely shot." After the Maple Leafs won the Stanley Cup in 1967, Sawchuk, who had played brilliantly in the deciding game, was physically and psychologically tortured to the point that he was incapable of celebrating with his teammates in the dressing room. Instead, he sat impassively in the corner, sucking mechanically on a cigarette, unable even to smile.

Gump Worsley once claimed that the demands of goaltending had driven him close to alcoholism.

Perhaps the most renowned case of "goaltender's nerves" belonged to Glenn Hall, an 11-time all-star with Detroit, Chicago and St. Louis during the 1950s and '60s. Hall's affliction was such that before every game, and often between periods, he would retire to the dressing room toilet for a vomiting session. If a spell of nerves caught up with him during play he would bang on the ice with his stick. Attuned and sympathetic to his pro-

1959

**Goaltender Terry Sawchuk** played on four Cup winners in 21 seasons. He is the only NHL goaltender to record more than 100 shutouts and, from 1951 to '55, allowed fewer than two goals-against per game.

blem, referees would temporarily halt a game while he visited the dressing room.

Other goaltenders have reacted more eccentrically to the rigors of the job. Gilles Gratton believed he was a reincarnated jungle cat and, according to Winnipeg Jets' general manager John Ferguson, once threw off his mask and gloves during a fight, began to growl, then skated up to an opposition player and pounced on him like a cat on a mouse.

Jacques Plante, who starred for the Canadiens during the 1950s and moved on to play in St. Louis, Toronto, Boston and New York, was less flamboyant in his eccentricity. Early in his career he is said to have enjoyed knitting as a way of calming his nerves. But his more significant idiosyncrasies affected the game itself. He was the first NHL goaltender, for instance, to wander beyond the goal crease and participate in the play. An excellent skater, he would often skate as far as 20 feet from his net to steer a loose puck into the corner or make a pass to a teammate. Montreal management, and numerous fans, reacted against his escapades at first, believing he was merely showboating; but it wasn't long before his participation in the play was recognized as an advantage and several other goaltenders adopted his roving habits. Plante once explained that his style was rooted in absolute practicality, not flakiness: "In semi-pro hockey I played behind a defense that had two guys who couldn't skate backwards and two who couldn't pivot. I could skate better than any of them so I started to skate out to clear loose pucks. That's how it started."

Plante was also the first goaltender regularly to wear a mask. Clint Benedict of the Montreal Maroons had temporarily worn one in 1927 but had abandoned it when he found that its nosepiece protruded too far to enable him to see pucks at his feet. During the autumn of 1959, Plante experimented in practice with a couple of masks, the most serviceable of which was a crude amalgam of opaque fiberglass and sponge rubber. He wore the latter in action for the first time on November 1, 1959, at Madison Square Garden, having been badly cut by a slapshot from Andy Bathgate. He never again played without it, and other goaltenders, too, were soon wearing masks. "If we hadn't done it," said Plante, "sooner or later somebody would have been killed playing goal."

Asked once for his assessment of a goaltender's lot, Plante replied, "Imagine yourself sitting in your office quietly doing your job. You make one little mistake, and suddenly a red light goes on over your head, and 15,000 people stand up and start screaming at you."

## Grinders and punch lines

Like most professions – medicine, law, advertising – hockey has generated its own unique vocabulary. The terms range from high-blown rhetoric to colorfully descriptive phrases, the best of which qualify as a kind of working poetry of the rink. The contemporary game is one of "grinders," of "roofed" shots, of goals scored from "the slot" and of players "hearing footsteps," "throwing snow," or "one-timing the puck." Players of an earlier era were sometimes said to "lay the hickory" to an opponent's shins – anything to prevent him from putting "the disc in the cage." Over the years, descriptions for the hockey stick have ranged the from simple "lumber" or "wood" to the "cudgel," "club" and "wand." The goal has been called everything from "the igloo," "twine" and "citadel" to the highly archaic "cord cottage" or "hempen hut."

Much of the game's more inventive terminology has been coined by the players themselves. Broadcasters and sportswriters, too, have contributed, creating some of the game's more onerous rhetoric and clichés as well as some of its more enduring phrases. Early in his career, broadcaster Foster Hewitt coined the classic exclamation, "He shoots, he scores!", which is still the definitive description of a puck being fired (whipped, rifled, smoked, driven, spanked) into a net. Hewitt's son, Bill, also a play-by-play announcer, eventually usurped the phrase, as have many other announcers. Today, the phrase is perhaps honored more in the breach than in practice, by announcers who deliberately avoid it as a measure of their individuality.

But it is still around the net that metaphor and turn-of-phrase are most frequently employed. A goal can be "banged" in, "tapped" in, "howled" in, or "rapped" in. A goaltender, having made a fine save, can be said to "stone", "blank" or "rob" opposing shooters.

At the more inflated end of the scale, Danny Gallivan's famous broadcasts of Montreal Canadiens' games were regularly laced with "cannonading drives," "blueline blasts" and descriptions of goaltenders thrusting out a pad in "rapier-like fashion." The esteemed broadcaster periodically used the word "spin-a-rama" to describe a puck carrier wheeling 360 degrees on the spot to avoid a checker. The move was often used by former Montreal defenseman Serge Savard, in which case it was a "Savardian spin-a-rama." Gallivan would occasionally describe a heroic player, particularly in a playoff series, as a "tower of strength"- or, in a moment of extreme adulation, a "Tower of Power."

Not all of the game's language has tended to inventiveness or hyperbole. Perhaps out of a desire to evade the probes of reporters, or to avoid tactical disclosures, some contemporary coaches have achieved an almost self-satirizing level of verbal predictability. Theirs is a world of players "coming to play every game" and "giving a hundred and ten percent," of teams "having the horses to get the job done." Not long ago, in describing how Team Canada '85 would play the Czech nationals in the World Hockey Championships, coach Doug Carpenter explained, "We can't open up on this ice surface. It's their ballpark. It will be kitty-bar-the-door hockey. We have to outsmart them, be overachievers. This is the run for the roses. We can't rest on our laurels. It's a one-game situation."

Other coaches and players have taken a more minimalist approach to discussing the game. Ted Green, who during the 1960s was a talented thumper with the Boston Bruins and is now an assistant coach with the Edmonton Oilers, invariably referred to his fights, whether minor scuffles or heinous punch-ups, as mere "involvements." If a fight in which he'd taken part was simply too gross to be accommodated by the euphemism, he would periodically stretch it to "quite an involvement."

Nowhere is the lingo of the game more recognizably embodied than in the nicknames that have been earned by the greats and others down through the decades: "the Stratford Streak" (Howie Morenz), "the Chicoutimi Cucumber" (Georges Vezina), "the Riverton Rifle" (Reggie Leach), "the Golden Jet" (Bobby Hull), Bernie "Boom-Boom" Geoffrion, "the Big M" (Frank Mahovlich), Larry "Big Bird" Robinson, "the Flower" (Guy Lafleur), Rick "Nifty" Middleton and "the Great Gretzky." In many cases, players' nicknames have become better known than their real names: "Red" Kelly, "Gump" Worsley, "King" Clancy, "Babe" Pratt, "Punch" Imlach, "Toe" Blake, "Turk" Broda, "Ace" Bailey, "Dit" Clapper, "Cyclone" Taylor, "Busher" Jackson, and of course "Rocket" Richard, or "Rock" as he was known in the dressing room. While some players have never incorporated their nicknames into their self-images, others have done so without hesitation. A brother of former Leaf Billy Harris once reported that, on answering a phone call for his brother who was not home, a small voice at the other end of the line had asked "Would you tell Billy that the Big M called?"

Forward lines, too, have earned enduring monickers, some of which have ballooned to legendary proportions in hockey lore. Mention of the

1939

**"The Kid Line** [above] was sensational. Charlie Conacher [left] was one of the great wrist-shooters in the game. Joe Primeau, the center, was a splendid playmaker and Busher Jackson [right] played hockey like ballet."
— *King Clancy*

The Kraut Line, left, was formed in 1938. Woody Dumart played on the left side, with Bobby Bauer on the right and Milt Schmidt at center. Boston won two Stanley Cups with the Krauts.

Kid Line (Primeau, Conacher and Jackson) to a veteran Toronto Maple Leaf fan will invariably bring a spark of recognition and nostalgia. Detroit's Production Line (Howe, Lindsay and Abel) or Montreal's Punch Line (Richard, Lach and Blake) will evoke similar recognition in those cities. Of more recent vintage are Buffalo's French Connection (Perreault, Robert and Martin) and Winnipeg's Tre Kronor (Steen, Lundholm and Lindstrom).

In rare instances, entire teams have been endowed with appropriate sobriquets. The Montreal Canadiens have long been "the Flying Frenchmen" or "Les Habitants" or simply "the Habs." In the early 1970s, the years of such resolute scrappers as Ted Green, Derek Sanderson and Wayne Cashman, the Boston Bruins became known as "the Big Bad Bruins."

**Wayne Gretzky** signed his first pro contract with the Indianapolis Racers of the WHA when he was 17. Gretzky played eight games for the Racers before joining Edmonton for the balance of the '77-'78 season.

Opposition players reluctant to meet them were sometimes said to have contracted "the Boston flu." A few years later, the Philadelphia Flyers became "the Broad Street Bullies." The Flyers had a number of excellent players – Bobby Clarke, Rick MacLeish, Bill Barber, Reggie Leach, Bernie Parent – but they also employed players paid primarily to put fear in the hearts of their opponents. The presence of intimidators such as Dave Shultz, Bob Kelly and Don Saleski tended to churn up the nastiness in other less bellicose Flyers, with the result that the team established several NHL records for most penalties received.

Almost since hockey's inception, good teams have had both flashy scorers and tough men. In every era of the sport, these team policemen have controlled the mood of individual games in order to provide opportunities for those players with a scoring touch to earn their pay. "Bad" Joe Hall, Eddie Shore, Ted Lindsay, Ted Green, John Ferguson, Tiger Williams, Dale Hunter and many others have faithfully performed this role throughout more than eighty years of organized hockey.

Conn Smythe, founder of the Maple Leafs, placed a premium on hockey players like Syl Apps and Hap Day whose play was characterized by both fairness and toughness. Certainly, there have been players in the game whose mere reputation of physical strength has kept would-be challengers in their place. Almost no NHLer in the 1950s or '60s, for instance, was willing to provoke Tim Horton or Gordie Howe. "I tried Horton once," said Derek Sanderson of the Bruins, "and he just put the bearhug on me. Never again."

### The expansion effect

In 1967, the NHL doubled from six to 12 teams, forever changing the shape of major-league hockey. Until then, the NHL had, for nearly 30 years, been an intimate, almost-fraternal organization. The league consisted of 120 players, all of whom played in six cities that were no more than an overnight train ride apart.

By 1972, major-league hockey had ballooned to an unwieldy, self-devastating 28 teams – 16 in the NHL and 12 in the WHA, with some 560 players in all. Junior and minor professional leagues, the traditional sources of skilled replacement players, had been drained of the players they could provide, and legitimate major-league talent was stretched to the point of transparency.

It would take nearly a decade before the Major Junior feeder system would even begin to adjust to the new demands on it. It would take the

1978

**The Birmingham Bulls and the Winnipeg Jets** were at opposite poles in the WHA in the 1970s. The Jets were a European-style team, while the Bulls mixed teenagers with some tough minor-league pros. Here Frank Beaton holds Jet Anders Hedberg.

NHL about the same period of time to clarify its vision of where it could advantageously "feed" to satisfy its now voracious appetite for qualified players.

Until the late 1960s, the Junior "A" leagues (ages 20 and under) had been the training grounds for virtually every player on any NHL team's roster. In any given year, only a few Juniors, the very cream of the talent, were called on to make, or were capable of making, the jump to the major leagues. If the Junior "A" leagues could produce even a dozen top graduates in a year, it was generally enough to keep the six-team NHL supplied with top-drawer personnel. Those who didn't make the jump immediately were often channeled to the minor-league pro teams where they gained experience that, in many cases, would equip them for eventual major-league play. Most pre-expansion players thought nothing of spending a year or two, or more, in the minor leagues.

Then came expansion, followed by the WHA, and suddenly every Junior player even half-equipped for pro hockey was hooked immediately into major-league service. What complicated things for the worse was that the WHA refused to honor an NHL rule which prohibited the drafting of Juniors before they had finished their last year of Junior eligibility at the age of 20. Anxious to scoop the best talent from its competitor, the new league began signing players at 17 or 18, or at as early an age as law would permit. During the mid-'70s, the Birmingham Bulls had as many as half a dozen 18- or 19-year-olds in their lineup – among them, Rob Ramage, Ken Linseman, Rick Vaive and Mark Napier, all of whom would go on to productive NHL careers. In 1978, Wayne Gretzky was signed at the age of 17 by the WHA's Indianapolis Racers.

### Final polish

To compensate for the haste with which Juniors were becoming front-line pros, at least one NHL team, the Montreal Canadiens, introduced an informal program of intensive skill-training for its younger players. Led by Claude Ruel (the training became known as Claude Ruel's Finishing School), the regular sessions subjected players to hour upon hour of basic drills: skating, passing, shooting, pass-receiving – any skills the Canadiens felt their young players were missing by short-circuiting the minor leagues or because of deficient training as Juniors. The young Guy Lafleur would stay on the ice with Ruel every day after practice, honing (among other skills) his deadly shot. Time after time he would storm in from the blueline, pick up Ruel's pass from the corner and blast the puck into the net. "*C'mon, Guy! C'mon, my Guy! Skate, my Guy!*" Ruel would

1970

**Guy Lafleur** scored 233 goals in his last two seasons of junior hockey with the Quebec Remparts.

**Toronto's Borje Salming** became the first European hockey player to star in the National Hockey League.

1983

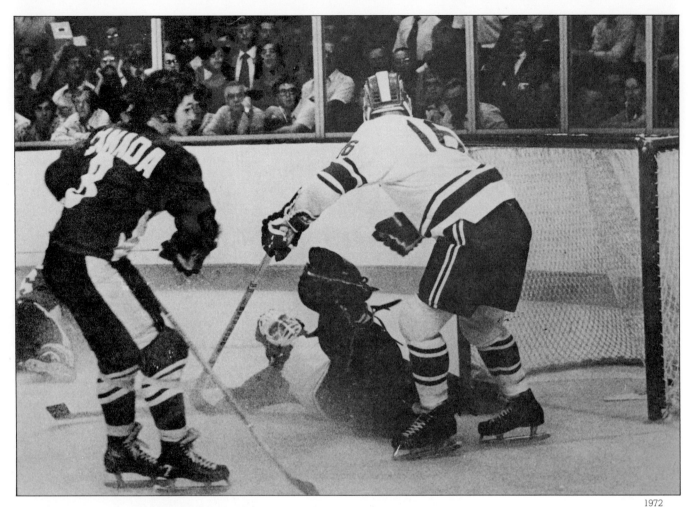

1972

**Game one, Team Canada vs. USSR:** "This moment was confirmation we were in for a difficult night. We scored in the first minute and then scored again, but soon the play began to even out. They scored once and then this goal tied the game. I remember Harry Sinden at the end of the period saying, 'You didn't think it was going to be easy, did you?' From the tone of his voice, as well as from everything else, you could tell that he was trying to persuade himself of that. And we were trying to persuade ourselves of the same thing, because to some extent we thought it *was* going to be easy." — *Ken Dryden*

coax, as he guided Lafleur through the exercises. If the Canadiens thought a player would benefit by it, the team was quite willing to buck the trend of the '70s and put the player through a season or more of minor-league hockey with its American League farm club, the Nova Scotia Voyageurs. All-stars Larry Robinson and Rod Langway were among the players to benefit from the added seasoning.

The Canadiens were one of few teams that refused, ever, to put intimidation ahead of traditional winning strategies; and it is not surprising or coincidental that when the time came, when "fright" hockey had reached its low ebb in the mid-'70s, it was the fast-skating, consummately trained Canadiens who were ready and waiting to return the game – or at least begin to return it – to its rightful skills and heirs. In 1976, the Canadiens regained the Stanley Cup from the Philadelphia Flyers and did not relinquish it for four years.

## New talent pools

Meanwhile, the NHL gradually evolved out of its dependence on junior hockey as its sole source of talent. By the mid-'70s, a number of top European players had started showing up in NHL uniforms – Borje Salming and Inge Hammarstrom in Toronto, Thommie Bergman and Vaclav Nedomansky in Detroit, Kent-Erik Andersson in Minnesota. More than any other early import, it was Borje Salming who proved to the skeptics that European players had much to contribute to the North American game. Far from wilting or turning the other cheek when his courage was tested by rugged NHL checkers, Salming took his lumps and gave them back in equal measure. During a couple of playoff series in the mid-'70s against the Philadelphia Flyers, the talented Swedish defenseman traded elbows and hostilities with the toughest of NHL pros and never so much as flinched. His stylish play earned him NHL all-star recognition six times between 1974 and 1980. He was the first European to be named an all-star and, until the selection of Jari Kurri of the Edmonton Oilers in 1983-'84, was the only European to be so honored.

By the late 1970s, there were numerous Europeans in the NHL, including some of the league's brightest stars; and most teams were doing serious scouting in Scandinavia and western Europe.

But it had been a WHA team, not an NHL team, that had most effectively shown the hockey world what Europeans could do in regular competition with North American pros. From the earliest years of their existence in the WHA, the Winnipeg Jets had scoured Sweden and Finland for fast-skating, highly skilled amateurs and semi-pros. At any time during the mid-to late '70s, the Jets had as many as nine or ten Scandinavians in their lineup – among them, Ulf Nilsson, Anders Hedberg, Lars Sjoberg, Dan Labraaten, Willy Lindstrom and Kent Nilsson, all of whom went on to play in the NHL, several of whom became stars.

By the late 1970s, major-league teams had realized that US college players, like the Europeans, had the skills and stamina necessary to flourish over a difficult, 80-game NHL regular season. As college-trained players came into the NHL, it was apparent that the coaching in the American (and some Canadian) colleges had gradually caught up with – and, in the view of many people, surpassed – that of the Junior leagues. What's more, there were instructional advantages to the campus milieu. Says former Minnesota North Star coach Glen Sonmor, "The athletes are in an educational setting, involved in the learning process all the time and, therefore, are very open to learning new things about hockey." Because the college schedule is only half the length of the typical Junior schedule, there is also far more time for skills instruction.

In spite of the apparent superiority of the college system, and, despite the increasing number of excellent players who graduate from it (Dave

1972
**Souvenir wooden puck** carries a caricature of Soviet scoring star Valeri Kharlamov.

Ellett, Rod Langway, Tom Kurvers, Chris Chelios, Ken Morrow et al), thus far the majority of top young NHL players continue to come out of Junior hockey (Denis Savard, Steve Yzerman, Wayne Gretzky, Mario Lemieux, Paul Coffey, Mark Messier, Tim Kerr and so on). It is, nonetheless, a measure of how the NHL has changed over the past 10 years that several clubs are now carrying as many as a dozen players from Europe and US college leagues. Even the Philadelphia Flyers who, as defending Stanley Cup champions in the mid-'70s, might have scoffed at such players, have a healthy proportion of Scandinavians, Czechs and American collegians on their roster. The Montreal Canadiens, perhaps the most tradition-conscious team in hockey, was one of the last clubs to utilize European imports. Today, Montreal is led offensively by a shifty, pint-sized Swede named Mats Naslund.

### Scaling the summit

Though it may have started as a response to the shortage of homegrown players, the NHL's adoption of Europeans was ultimately powered by a far richer imperative: the realization that, at the international and top club levels, European hockey in the 1970s was on a virtual par with the North American professional game. In fact, in some ways it was *ahead* of our game.

The beginning of this realization came in 1972, in the now-legendary series between Canada's NHL all-stars and the national team of the Soviet Union. Up to this point, the NHL hadn't involved itself in international hockey. After all, what could it possibly gain by playing the Soviets? When, finally, the 1972 series was arranged, nearly everyone connected to Canadian hockey expected a Team Canada victory of embarrassing proportions. Even so, on September 2, 1972, if only out of curiosity, we gathered by our television sets. Our expectations were soon confirmed, as Phil Esposito fired an easy goal past Vladislav Tretiak only 30 seconds into the game. Six minutes later it was 2-0, and some of us found ourselves quietly hoping that the Canadians would not go too hard on the visitors, that the Russians would at least be able to save face.

Before the end of the period, they had done exactly that, tying the score 2-2. By the end of the next period, with the Soviets up 4-2, it was all we could do to hope numbly that the Canadians would be able to save face. Early in the third period, Bobby Clarke temporarily raised our hopes with a goal, but by the final buzzer the Soviets had scored three more times for a relatively easy 7-3 victory.

North American hockey fans were stunned. And although Team Canada went on to win the series by the slimmest of margins, it was clearly realized that North American hockey had fallen behind the Soviet game in a number of vital aspects. They were better and faster skaters than we were. They were better passers; they seemed stronger, better conditioned, better disciplined. They were more creative in their passing and skating patterns. What's more, their style simply looked more interesting than ours. The only areas of undeniable Canadian superiority were the mucking and grinding aspects of the game and sheer determination, which, as the series wound down in Moscow, Team Canada possessed in ever-increasing abundance. But even Paul Henderson's famous series-winning goal, with 34 seconds left in the eighth and deciding game, provided only temporary ecstasy for Canadian fans. It was already understood that if we didn't adjust our game, and adjust it quickly, the Soviets, and possibly other top European teams, would eventually leave us in their wake.

It wasn't that we mightn't have seen the excellence of the Soviets coming. As early as 1954, they defeated Canada for their first World Amateur

**Soviet Boris Mikhailov** and US goalie Jim Craig. "The 1980 US Olympic gold-medal victory proved what nationalism, heart and guts can do when inspired coaching convinces a bunch of college players that they're superstars."
— *George Gross*

1980

Championship, a title that, up to then, Canada had been able to win by sending even a passable Senior "A" team to the competition. By the mid-1960s, not even our best amateurs or minor-league pros could stay with them. In the late 1960s, Father David Bauer trained several elite Canadian amateur teams for Olympic and world competition; but even with months of intensive preparation, the teams were no match for the more experienced Soviets. Nonetheless, nothing we had seen before 1972 could have quite prepared us for the dramatic revelations of that year's summit.

In retrospect, that series demonstrated that hockey was truly a world game and that the best from Europe and the best from North America had a lot to learn from one another. The NHL saw how effective a rapid-movement style can be when executed by well-coached and conditioned players; the Soviets saw how heart and tenacity can break down even the most systematic approach to hockey.

In 1976, a second Team Canada defeated the Soviets and Czechs in Canada Cup play; but in 1979, a brash young team from the Soviet Union took on the NHL all-stars in a three-game series in New York and beat them decisively. Though the NHL team won the first game, the Soviets rallied in the second and won the third game by an embarrassing 6-0 score. They did not allow the NHL a single goal in the concluding 95 minutes of the series.

The Soviets won a subsequent Canada Cup tournament in 1981; but by 1984, the Canadian game had renewed itself to the point that Team Canada was once again able to return the Canada Cup to its home country. In the 1985 World Championships in Prague, Canada's entry – an agglomeration of players who had been eliminated from the NHL playoffs – again showed well, defeating the Soviets, but narrowly losing the title to the Czechs.

### Icy miracle

In much the same way that the aforementioned series have legitimized European hockey in the minds of North Americans, the American victory at the 1980 Olympics in Lake Placid – the so-called Miracle on Ice – gave a new glitter and credibility to US college hockey. Relentlessly, shrewdly prepared by coach Herb Brooks, the young American Olympians surpassed not only the powerful Czech, Swedish and Canadian Olympic teams but the national team of the Soviet Union, the same team that, a year earlier, had conquered the NHL all-stars. The victory was achieved by enormous ambition coupled with a number of significant technical factors: excellent passing and checking, good team speed, and a sound puck-control or possession game – a refusal merely to dump the puck into the opposition's end of the rink and chase after it. "I didn't want the team throwing the puck away with no reason," said Brooks. "That's stupid. It's the same as punting on first down. The style I wanted combined the determined checking of the North American game and the best features of the European game."

That a number of players on the American team have gone on to successful NHL careers – Ken Morrow, Mike Ramsey, Mark Pavelich, Steve Christoff, Dave Christian, Jack O'Callahan and Mark Johnson – is strong evidence that US college hockey has achieved parity (in quality, if not yet quantity, of graduates to the NHL) with any other training ground in the world.

The more recent 1984 US Olympic program also produced several NHL players, notably Al Iafrate, Chris Chelios, Ed Olczyk, Pat Lafontaine and Marc Behrend. The Canadian Olympic program, too, has been a source of highly regarded NHL players. The 1980 and '84 teams' alumni include Glenn Anderson, Kirk Muller, Craig Redmond, Pat Flatley and Russ Courtnall, to name but a few.

## The modern speed game

Generally speaking, the NHL has responded enthusiastically to the influences and challenges of the past dozen years. In the words of Calgary Flames' general manager Cliff Fletcher, "When we saw the way the Soviet national team played the game, their beautiful passing plays with the puck always going to a player who was on the move, and the way all players on the ice were involved in their plays, it was drilled home to us that our game needed some changes."

Former NHL coach Fred Shero said, "The Europeans and Soviets play such an entertaining brand of hockey with so much skating and passing skill that it was natural NHL teams wanted to play that way. They showed us that total team play is the easiest way to do it, that by passing the puck and being on the move all the time, a team can get up the ice much more easily than by individual rushes."

The average NHL team of the 1980s puts far more emphasis on offense, on scoring goals, than it did 10 or 20 years ago. That's not to say that the purpose of the game hasn't always been to score goals; but during the '50s and '60s there was a far greater emphasis on *preventing* goals. The goals-against average of the Edmonton Oilers in their first championship season, 1983-'84, was nearly four per game. The goals-against average of the championship Toronto Maple Leafs of 20 years earlier had been less than 2.5 per game. Even more noteworthy is that the '83-'84 Oilers *scored* an average of 5.5 goals per game, while the '63-'64 Maple Leafs scored less than half that many. Reactionary observers have been inclined to see the less defensive style as a weakness of the contemporary game; but from a fan's point of view it couldn't be better, inasmuch as the production of a goal is almost always more exciting than the prevention of one. It is also entirely possible that, with the greater motion and speed of today's game, goals are simply more difficult to prevent than they were under the older more rigid patterns of play.

Today's game is remarkably fast. Not only do most contemporary players pass the puck more and carry it less, but they also have become better skaters wearing lighter equipment. Coaches have responded to this fast pace by rotating their forwards and defensemen more frequently. During the '50s and '60s, players were regularly on the ice for two minutes or more during a shift. Today's lines are changed as frequently as once a minute.

Conditioning has improved, too. It wasn't long ago that the average NHL player reported to training camp in early September, skated for an hour or so a day, participated in a few scrimmages and exhibition games, and considered himself ready for action. Players were often said to be "playing themselves into shape." Today's conditioning goes on year round, and many players have individually tailored programs of off-season training. When it was realized that the Soviets could fend off most NHL players with one arm, North American teams also began putting more emphasis on upper-body strength. The result has been that numerous players now participate in regular weight-training programs.

With increased focus on speed and conditioning, it's not surprising that the average NHL player is now five years younger than the average player of the 1960s. Players come into the league younger and retire younger. The average age of a Philadelphia Flyer during the '84-'85 season was approximately 24 years. Ten years earlier, the team average was nearly 29 years.

NHL coaching, too, has evolved steadily over the past dozen years. In the pre-expansion era – a time when baseball and football teams were customarily employing up to four coaches per team – no NHL team employed more than one coach; and the chief qualification for the job was NHL playing experience. The old six-team league had a successful product, and the relatively few men who controlled that product saw no reason to alter it. At any rate, what would a second coach do? Wasn't one coach enough to motivate the players and change the lines?

In today's 21-team league, there are some 50 full-time coaches, a number of whom have special qualifications in physical education or psychology. Some teams use fitness consultants and some employ special goaltending coaches. During games, certain clubs have taken to putting an assistant coach in the press box to identify and analyze on-ice developments and relay observations to the bench. Says Scotty Bowman who, with Roger Neilson, pioneered the system for the Buffalo Sabres, "If the other team throws something new at you and you don't recognize it,

1979

**Gordie Howe's 35-year career** in professional hockey brought him the great thrill of playing in the WHA and the NHL with his two sons Mark, left, and Marty, right.

your club can be down a couple of goals by the end of the period. The spotter can pass the information along to the second coach at the bench right away, and you can make adjustments."

## Salary expansion

One of the greatest changes in the modern game has taken place not on the ice but at the bank, where some players now deposit nearly as much money per game as players of 30 years ago could hope to deposit in a year. Ted Green said recently, "When I signed with the Bruins in 1960, they gave me a $7,500 salary and $500 as a signing bonus. People say that was a lot of money back then, but the heck it was – it was nothing! I was keeping residences in both Winnipeg and Boston. I had to travel between both cities. Even in the late '60s, if an all-star was making twenty to twenty-five thousand, it was big money. Back then, you made a buck, you lived, you raised a family, you put a few dollars aside. That was about it. I went a long time before I made a good buck with the Bruins in 1972."

The significance of the year 1972 to Green and to dozens of other players was the founding of the WHA, which came on the scene with an unprecedented display of spending. Bobby Hull and Derek Sanderson were coaxed away from the Black Hawks and Bruins and signed to multi-million-dollar contracts by the new league. Even journeyman players, who might have been earning $20,000 in the NHL, were given $100,000 contracts by WHA teams. The new league needed fans, and the quickest way to get them was by hiring recognizable players. The monetary opportunity, plus the chance to play with his sons, Mark and Marty, was enough to bring Gordie Howe out of retirement to sign with the Houston Aeros.

NHL owners eventually decided that the only way to end the highly attritional bidding war was to incorporate what remained of the WHA into the NHL, which they did in 1979, to the great relief of both sides. At the time, NHL president John Ziegler said, "For the past eight years, just about the only subject discussed in our board of governors' meetings has been survival. We've talked on and on and on about our legal action against the other league, the collective bargaining agreement with the Players' Association, the financial problems of many of our teams and the gigantic escalation in salaries. One thing we just haven't found time to discuss very often is the caliber of play on the ice and what we might do to improve it."

It wasn't long before improvements began to take place. And they have continued, so that today, six years later, the NHL is the finest aggregation of hockey players – and the highest *paid* aggregation – in the history of the sport.

### A fan's game

But hockey, finally, is more than a game for talented pros with large contracts playing in cavernous arenas. It is a game for church teams and school teams and pick-up teams. It is a game for middle-aged men playing in small arenas at odd hours of the night – without spectators and without pay; a game for small-time pros traveling long distances by bus over icy rural roads. It is a game for boys and girls who gather on neighborhood rinks or frozen rivers or farm ponds or in barely heated arenas in small towns, often before sunrise, when ice time is available.

As much as for anyone, hockey is a game for its fans. If it weren't, why the vast numbers of seats in big-league arenas? Why the millions of dollars' worth of publicity, the sports pages, the Hall of Fame? Why the enormous television contracts?

Hockey is our game; it belongs to us as much as to the players, coaches or administrators. For every one of them, there are 10,000 of us.

For those of us who were raised on the sport and love it, it is, as writer-broadcaster Peter Gzowski said in the title of his book, *The Game of Our Lives.* We choose our teams and commit a portion of ourselves to them. And, in turn, they come to represent us, reflecting our best hopes, as well as the many other expressions of our existence: our frustrations, anxieties and antipathies.

I remember as a child being so caught up in pivotal playoff games, televised games, that I was unable to stay in the room with the television, for fear something disastrous would happen to my team, the Maple Leafs. My mother, the other great fan in our family, one who seldom missed a broadcast, would remind me sympathetically that it was "only a game." Yet when the opposition scored an important goal, it was invariably she, not I, who was first to voice her dismay. "Surely not!" I remember her gasping.

I once read that, during the deciding game of the 1963 Stanley Cup finals, Maple Leaf owner Stafford Smythe had, like myself, been unable to stand the tension and had walked out of the Gardens and along Toronto's Carlton Street until the game was over. I have heard of injured players who have been unable to watch their teammates struggle through the fortunes and misfortunes of Stanley Cup competition.

Hockey draws us in, fascinates us, astonishes us, enrages us; it obsesses and thrills us.

Hockey is drama. And perhaps for more than any other reason, that is why we watch it.

*– Charles Wilkins*

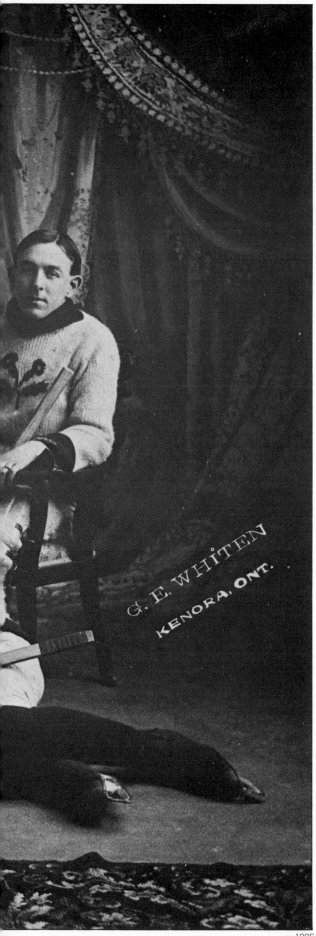

# ORIGINS: THE YEARS TO 1926

G. E. WHITEN
KENORA, ONT.

c. 1905

**In hockey's earliest years,** the game progressed rapidly. Its rules were codified, and fan interest sparked the formation of professional teams employing the game's first stars.

The Rat Portage (Kenora, Ontario) Thistles display the Amateur Hockey Association of Canada senior championship trophy. They went on to win the Stanley Cup in January 1907, after unsuccessful challenges in 1903 and 1905.

c. 1885

**Pond hockey** in Saskatchewan. Note the tree branches used as sticks.

c. 1905

1893

**The Montreal Amateur Athletic Association** won the Stanley Cup the first year the trophy was presented. MAAA compiled a 7-1 won-lost record over the 10-week season, winning the Cup. Only in this inaugural year was the Cup awarded without some sort of playoff series separate from regular season play.

*Top row,* from left: Alex Irving, Haviland Routh, Allan Cameron. *Middle row:* unidentified, James Stewart, A.B. Kingan. *Front row:* J. Lowe, T. Paton, Archie Hodgson, Billy Barlow.

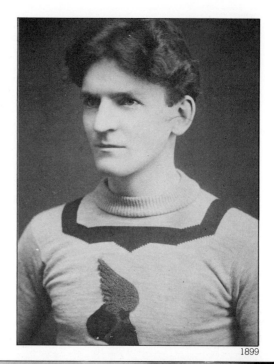

**Montreal Shamrocks won the 1899 Stanley Cup.**
In these early years, aspiring Cup-holders issued
challenges to the team that held the trophy. A board of
trustees examined each challenger's credentials and,
if accepted, scheduled a playoff for the Cup. The
Shamrocks defeated Queen's University 6-2 in a one-
game final.

  Harry Trihey, right, was the scoring star of the
Shamrocks, with 19 goals in seven regular-season games.

  *Front row,* from left: C. Hoerner, Fred Scanlon, Harry Trihey, Jack
Brannen. *Top row:* J. McKenna, unidentified, Frank Tansey, C. Foley,
D. Dunphy, Frank Wall, Arthur Farrell.

1899

1899

c. 1906

c. 1907

**The Wanderers,** another Montreal club, won the Stanley Cup four times between 1906 and 1910.

Ernie "Moose" Johnson, left, began his career as a speedy left winger before being shifted to defense. He was a big man who used a very long stick, making it difficult for his opponents to get past him.

In 1912, he left the Wanderers to join his former teammate Lester Patrick, above, in the Pacific Coast league. Patrick was captain of the Wanderers in 1906 and 1907, before moving west where he coached, managed and played until 1926.

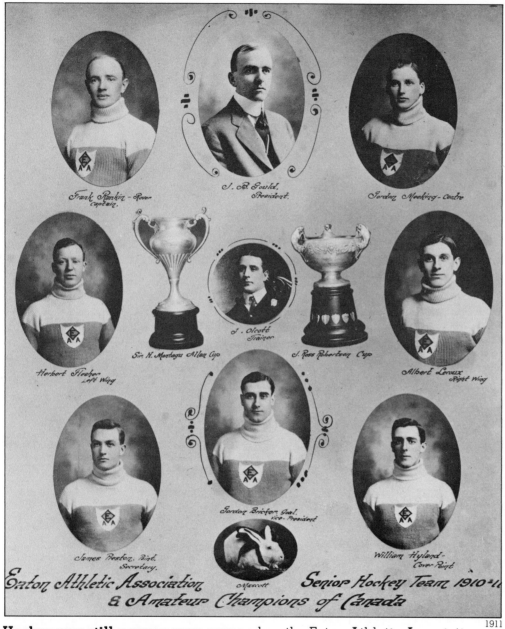

Eaton Athletic Association & Amateur Champions of Canada
Senior Hockey Team 1910-11

1911

**Hockey was still a seven-man game** when the Eaton Athletic Association won the Ontario amateur championship in 1911 and 1912. The seventh man was a rover and often the best athlete on the team. This photograph states that the Eaton club won the Allan Cup as Canadian amateur champions but, in fact, this team lost in the finals to the Winnipeg Victorias. Note the mascot.

1924

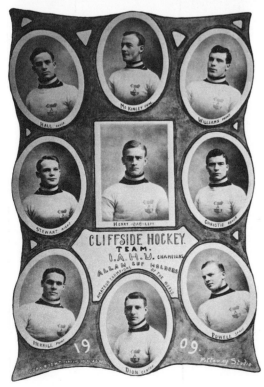

1909

**Senior amateur hockey** attracted enthusiastic support and groomed many players for the professional game. This larger-than-life replica celebrated the Soo (Sault Ste. Marie, Ontario) Greyhounds' Allan Cup victory in 1924. Fred "Bun" Cook from this Soo team joined his brother, Bill, and Frank Boucher on one of the NHL's top lines with the New York Rangers in the 1930s.

The first winners of the Allan Cup were the Ottawa Cliffsides who won in 1908-'09.

**Paddy Moran** tended goal for the Quebec (City) Bulldogs for all but one season between 1901 and 1917. He played the stand-up style common at this time and was part of two Stanley Cup teams in the successive years 1912 and 1913.

**In the game's early years,** numerous leagues formed, amalgamated and disbanded. By the time the Quebec Bulldogs successfully challenged for the Stanley Cup, the National Hockey Association in eastern Canada and the Pacific Coast Hockey Association in the West competed for the services of the best players.

The NHA champion was awarded the O'Brien Cup, left, which was constructed from solid silver mined in the boom towns that were home to some of hockey's first professional teams.

1913

**The Bulldogs won the 1913 Stanley Cup** by defeating the Sydney (Nova Scotia) Millionaires 14-3 and 6-3. Phantom Joe Malone scored nine goals in the first game of the final.
*Standing,* from left: D. Beland, Billy Creighton, Walter Rooney, Jeff Malone, M. Quinn. *Seated,* from left: Tommy Smith, Rusty Crawford, Paddy Moran, Joe Malone, Joe Hall, Jack Marks and Harry Mummery.

**By 1915 some of hockey's biggest stars** had been hired away from eastern clubs to play in the Pacific Coast Hockey Association. For the 1915 season, the PCHA fielded three teams: Vancouver Millionaires, Portland Rosebuds and Victoria Aristocrats.

The PCHA played with seven men on the ice; the NHA with six. In the Stanley Cup final, two of three games were played under western rules.

Vancouver's Frank Nighbor, right, scored five goals in the final. Nighbor was famous for gentlemanly play and for his ability to poke-check opposing players. Playing most of his career with the Ottawa Senators, he was also one of hockey's first 200-goal scorers.

**The Vancouver Millionaires, Stanley Cup champions, 1914-'15.** *Front row,* left to right: manager Frank Patrick, Si Griffis, Lloyd Cook, Hugh Lehman. *Top row:* Barney Stanley, Cyclone Taylor, unidentified, Mickey Mackay, Frank Nighbor.

c. 1910

1911

**Jack Darragh** was on four Cup-winners in 13 seasons with Ottawa. He had a great backhand shot and was known as a player who got important goals.

1911

**Art Ross** played for six clubs from 1905 to 1918, later becoming a manager, coach and hockey innovator. His efforts established the game in Boston.

1910

**C. Toms,** appears in the uniform of the Cobalt Silver Kings, who played in the NHA in 1910. The Kings won four and lost eight in their only season.

1911

**Georges Vezina** is considered to be one of the finest goaltenders of all time. Here he wears an early version of the Canadiens uniform.

1910

**Jack Laviolette** managed the first edition of the Montreal Canadiens in 1910. He was a speedster and one of the first great rushing defensemen.

1910

**Forward Horace Gaul** had 22 goals in 12 games for Haileybury in the NHA. He was a late addition to Ottawa's Cup-winning team in 1905.

1911

**Percy LeSueur** played goal for Ottawa from 1906 to 1913. After retiring in 1916, he served as a referee, coach, manager and broadcaster.

1911

**Cyclone Taylor** starred with Ottawa and Renfrew in the East and Vancouver in the West. He scored many goals as a rover in seven-man hockey.

1924

**"Babe Dye could shoot** a puck like a bullet. He played with Toronto St. Pats when I played with Ottawa. He was a great baseball player, too."
— *King Clancy*

Dye was an expert stickhandler with a hard shot from right wing. In the early 1920s, he was the NHL's leading scorer on four occasions. In his best year, 1922-'23, he had 41 goals in 31 regular season and playoff games.

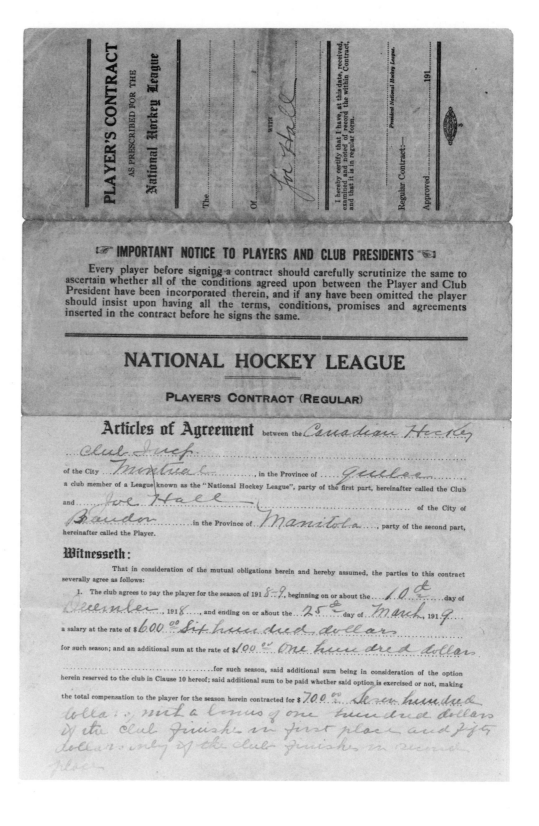

PLAYER'S CONTRACT

AS PRESCRIBED FOR THE

National Hockey League

The

Of

WITH

Joe Hall

I hereby certify that I have, at this date, received, examined and noted of record the within Contract, and that it is in regular form.

President National Hockey League.

Regular Contract:—

Approved

191

**IMPORTANT NOTICE TO PLAYERS AND CLUB PRESIDENTS**

Every player before signing a contract should carefully scrutinize the same to ascertain whether all of the conditions agreed upon between the Player and Club President have been incorporated therein, and if any have been omitted the player should insist upon having all the terms, conditions, promises and agreements inserted in the contract before he signs the same.

# NATIONAL HOCKEY LEAGUE

### PLAYER'S CONTRACT (REGULAR)

**Articles of Agreement** between the Canadian Hockey Club Inch

of the City Montreal , in the Province of Quebec

a club member of a League known as the "National Hockey League", party of the first part, hereinafter called the Club

and Joe Hall of the City of

Brandon in the Province of Manitoba , party of the second part, hereinafter called the Player.

**Witnesseth:**

That in consideration of the mutual obligations herein and hereby assumed, the parties to this contract severally agree as follows:

1. The club agrees to pay the player for the season of 1918-9, beginning on or about the 10th day of December, 1918, and ending on or about the 25th day of March, 1919

a salary at the rate of $600.00 Six hundred dollars

for such season; and an additional sum at the rate of $100.00 One hundred dollars

for such season, said additional sum being in consideration of the option herein reserved to the club in Clause 10 hereof; said additional sum to be paid whether said option is exercised or not, making

the total compensation to the player for the season herein contracted for $700.00 Seven hundred dollars, with a bonus of one hundred dollars if the club finishes in first place and fifty dollars only if the club finishes in second place.

c. 1913

**"Bad" Joe Hall** was considered one of the top defensemen and roughest players in the NHA. He played for the Quebec Bulldogs from 1911 to 1917 before joining Montreal in the newly formed NHL. With Montreal, he traveled to Seattle for the 1919 Stanley Cup finals. There he died of influenza, part of an epidemic that forced cancellation of the series.

The contract at left was Joe Hall's last.

c. 1910

**Conn Smythe was captain** of the University of Toronto Varsity hockey club that won the Ontario junior championship in 1915. The 1914 Varsity club lost only one game, an exhibition match with the Carlyle Indians who had super-athlete Jim Thorpe on their roster. Later, Smythe became an NHL coach, manager, sports entrepreneur and builder of the Toronto Maple Leaf franchise.

c. 1920

c. 1920

**The stylish play of Didier Pitre** combined with that of Jack Laviolette to establish the tradition of skill and speed that has characterized the Montreal Canadiens since the franchise began in 1910. Pitre's hard shot connected for 240 goals between 1904 and 1923.

**Until 1922,** goaltenders in the NHL were not permitted to drop to their knees to stop a shot. The accepted style was to play with both hands holding a long goal stick that was used to sweep the puck out of harm's way.

Georges Vezina was one of the league's steadiest goaltenders and one of the best at the stand-up style. He played every regular season and playoff game for Montreal from the time he broke into the NHL in 1911 until illness forced his retirement in 1926. During these years, the Canadiens won the league championship five times and the Stanley Cup twice.

Today, Vezina's name connotes excellence in the nets. The annual award to the NHL's top goaltender is known as the Vezina Trophy.

1924

**Montreal won the Stanley Cup** in 1924, largely on the strength of a forward line that combined Ottawa-born Aurel Joliat at left wing with Howie Morenz and Billy Boucher. Joliat and Morenz, a center, would play together with various right wingers for 11 seasons.

Joliat was an elusive skater who weighed less than 140 pounds. His speed and small stature allowed him to avoid opposing checkers and remain one of the top forwards in hockey until the late 1930s.

**Joe Malone's great hockey career** ended in Montreal just when Joliat and Morenz emerged as top players. Malone was prominent with Quebec, serving as captain of the Bulldogs for seven seasons. In 1917-'18, the first year of the NHL, he scored 44 goals in 20 games. This record remained unbroken until 1945, when Rocket Richard scored 50 goals in 50 games.

1924

1926

c. 1921

**The Stanley Cup left Canada** for the first time in 1917 when the Seattle Metropolitans of the PCHA defeated Montreal three games to one to win the championship. Mets goalie Happy "Hap" Holmes allowed 11 goals over the four games of the final. Holmes also played for Toronto, Victoria and, when this photograph was taken, Detroit.

Seattle's top checking forward was Jack Walker, left. He played in the PCHA and its successor, the Western Canada Hockey League, until declining fan interest and expansion into the US by the NHL combined to make the NHL the world's major professional league. By 1927, the best western players were playing in the NHL.

1922

**Barney Stanley** played and coached for 11 seasons in the PCHA and WCHL. In his rookie season he was part of the Stanley Cup winning Vancouver Millionaires of 1915. Stanley and Hugh Lehman, goalie for Vancouver, combined to coach the Chicago Black Hawks in 1927-'28, that franchise's second year in the NHL.

**Cleaning the ice in Ottawa.**

1922

c. 1930

# ESTABLISHMENT YEARS: 1927 TO 1946

**Members of the Detroit Falcons** pass the puck in a practice drill. During the years 1927-1946, hockey evolved from a stickhandling game to a passing one. As professional hockey became established, rules governing forward passing, offside infractions, player substitutions and icing the puck were modified to increase the pace of the game and enhance spectator appeal.

c. 1930

**As an amateur, Hooley Smith** played on Canada's 1924 Olympic team. In the NHL he had the good fortune to play with splendid linemates: Cy Denneny and Frank Nighbor in Ottawa and Nels Stewart and Babe Siebert in Montreal.

1935

**Conn Smythe was intent** on building a powerful Toronto team in 1930 when he purchased a talented defenseman named King Clancy from Ottawa for the unheard-of price of $35,000 and two players. Smythe raised the remaining $10,000 of this sum by betting on a long-shot winner at the racetrack. Here he talks with, from left, Clancy, Red Horner, Flash Hollet and George Hainsworth.

"To Conn Smythe, hockey was sacred. He lived for the game and was a tremendous patriot."
— *Camil DesRoches*

1931

**"Les Canadiens sont là!"** reads the window display celebrating Montreal's second consecutive Cup win in 1931. This was a colorful team built around the exploits of Howie Morenz, Aurel Joliat, Pit Lepine and others. Leo Dandurand, bottom right, joined with two partners in buying the Canadiens franchise for $11,000 in 1921. He then built a crowd-pleasing team that commanded tremendous loyalty from its fans.

c. 1933

1932

**Ching Johnson,** top left, and Taffy Abel, above, were two of the first big men in the game. Both were well over 200 pounds in an era when most players weighed at least fifty pounds less. They formed a huge defense pair for the New York Rangers when that franchise first entered the NHL in 1927.

Clint Benedict, here wearing a leather mask to protect an earlier injury, starred with Ottawa and the Montreal Maroons.

"I once scored a goal against Benedict with seven seconds to go in a game. He was playing for the Maroons and I was playing for Ottawa. Just to get rid of the puck, I let a shot go from way out and it went right in, putting us ahead 1-0. I went down and said something to him and he just said, 'Get out of here.' "
— *King Clancy*

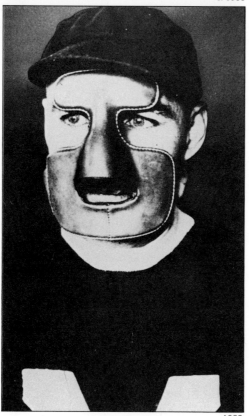

1928

c. 1933

**Dick Irvin, Sr.** coached in the NHL for 25 years after retiring as a player in 1929. He coached the Maple Leafs from 1931 to 1940, and the Canadiens from 1940 to 1955.

"He was a tremendous competitor. I traveled with Dick and the team to all the out-of-town games for nine years. I saw that like all the great coaches, he lived, ate and dreamt hockey. When we would go into Boston or Detroit he would always have a subject ready to discuss with the newspapermen. He'd stir things up. If it was an ordinary game, he'd make it a big game. He was always working to motivate his players." — *Camil DesRoches*

**The Toronto Maple Leafs won the Stanley Cup** in 1931-'32 with a team that featured the Kid Line and steady defense. The newly constructed Maple Leaf Gardens allowed crowds of more than 14,000 to witness the Leafs defeat the New York Rangers in three consecutive games to win the final. Enthusiasm for the team prompted photo cartoons in which the Leafs were depicted as a racing locomotive (top), a charging cavalry and an artillery battery.

**The Toronto Maple Leafs, Stanley Cup champions, 1931-'32.** *Front row,* left to right: Charlie Conacher, Joe Primeau, King Clancy, Frank Selke, Conn Smythe, Dick Irvin, Hap Day, Ace Bailey, Busher Jackson. *Top row:* Harold Darragh, Tim Daly, Alex Levinsky, Red Horner, Andy Blair, Lorne Chabot, Harold Cotton, Bob Gracie, Ken Doraty.

1932

1932

1932

1934

**The first NHL all-star game** was played to raise money
for Leaf player Ace Bailey who had been severely injured
when his head struck the ice after being hit from behind
by Eddie Shore, right. Toronto, wearing blue uniforms
with the word "ACE" emblazoned across the chest,
played the all-stars, who wore orange uniforms with
black trim. Toronto won 7-3.

1933

**The ice,** without painted goal-lines or face-off circles, looks bare in this game between Boston and the New York Rangers. Tiny Thompson is the Boston goalie.

1938

**Manager Red Dutton** greets Lorne Carr, whose goal after 60 minutes of overtime eliminated the Americans' rivals, the Rangers, from the playoffs.

1938

1933

1933

**In 1920, hockey was a winter Olympic sport** and was being played internationally by European and North American teams. In 1933, the world amateur championship was won by the United States, bottom, with Czechoslovakia, top, finishing third.

1930

**This program cover** depicts a game between Toronto and the Montreal Maroons. Players from other clubs observe from the first row of seats. Note the referee's handbell, visible in the top left corner of the ice. Artist Lou Skuce became well known for his hockey caricatures.

LA PRESSE, MONTREAL, SAMEDI 3 JANVIER 1931

**Johnny GOTTSELIG** Ce brillant joueur d'attaque du Chicago de la Ligue Nationale est âgé de 25 ans. Il mesure cinq pieds et onze pouces et pèse 152 livres. Il est réputé pour sa rapidité, son esprit combattif et ses manières toutes sportives.

1931

**Johnny Gottselig played for the Chicago Black Hawks** throughout his 15-year career. He was part of two Stanley Cup teams in 1933-'34 and 1937-'38. He was a dextrous stickhandler, winning all-star recognition in 1939. After retiring in 1945, he coached the Hawks for three seasons.

LA PRESSE, MONTREAL, SAMEDI 5 JANVIER 1929

**BABE SIEBERT**

L'un des piliers de la défense du Montréal, et l'un des plus rapides joueurs de la ligue professionnelle, Siebert est un artiste du hockey. Il est l'un des hommes les plus brillants et les plus effectifs sur le club de M. James Strachan.

1929

**Babe Siebert's playing career saw him excel** first as a forward on the "S Line" with Nels Stewart and Hooley Smith for the Montreal Maroons, and then as a defenseman for the Rangers, Bruins and Canadiens. He won the Hart Trophy as most valuable player with the Canadiens in 1937.

LA PRESSE, MONTREAL, SAMEDI 2 JANVIER 1932

## GEORGE OWEN

Le capitaine du club de hockey Boston est l'un des bons joueurs de défense de la N. H. L. et l'un des meilleurs hommes du club d'Art. Ross. Non seulement, il est solide et effectif dans son territoire, mais il est aussi très agressif et ses passes aux joueurs d'attaque ont permis à ces derniers de compter nombre de beaux points. Owen est un joueur très précieux.

1932

**George Owen grew up in the Boston area** and was captain of the Harvard Varsity team in 1921 and 1922. He stayed in Boston to pursue business interests, finally signing with the Bruins at age 26 in 1928. He played defense paired, at times, with stars Eddie Shore and Lionel Hitchman.

LA PRESSE, MONTREAL, SAMEDI 20 DECEMBRE 1930

**JOHNNY GAGNON** Ce jeune joueur d'aile droite, élégant et rapide patineur, est la seule recrue que le club de hockey Canadien présente sur l'alignement de son équipe cette saison. Gagnon a été l'une des figures dominantes du Providence de la Ligue Canadienne-Américaine, la saison dernière.

1930

**Johnny "Black Cat" Gagnon was on a Stanley Cup winner** in his rookie season with Montreal in 1930-'31. At five-foot-five and 140 pounds, he played a speedy right wing on a line with Howie Morenz and Aurel Joliat. His best year was 1936-'37, when he led the team with 36 points.

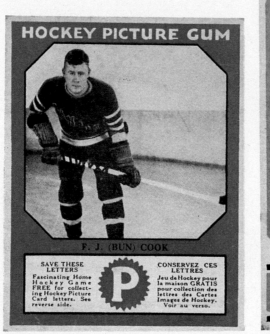

1933

1933

**Bun Cook** was an original member of the New York Rangers. He played 10 years, winning the Cup in 1928 and 1933.

**Ken Doraty** scored the winner for Toronto after 104 minutes of overtime against Boston in the 1933 playoffs.

1933

1937

**Nels Stewart's** career total of 324 goals topped all players of his era. He twice won the league's MVP award.

**Charlie Conacher** was a five-time all-star as the right wing on the Leafs' potent "Kid Line" in the 1930s.

WALTER GALBRAITH

1933

**Perk Galbraith** played left wing for the Boston Bruins from 1927 to 1934. He was 28 when he first played in the NHL.

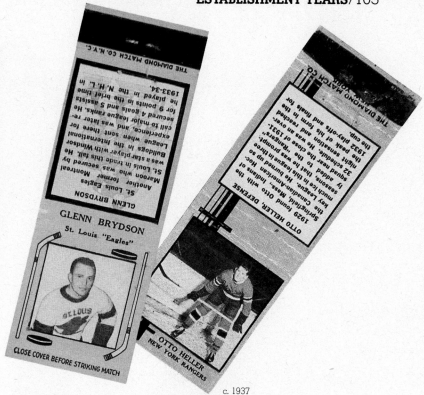

c. 1937

**Ott Heller** played 15 seasons with the Rangers. **Glen Brydson** played for the Leafs, Canadiens, Rangers, St. Louis Eagles and Black Hawks.

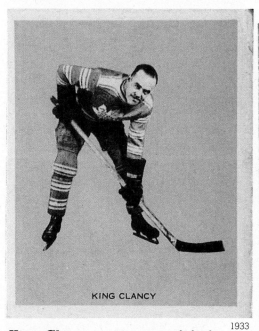

KING CLANCY

1933

**King Clancy** was a rugged, little sparkplug defenseman with the Ottawa Senators and the Toronto Maple Leafs from 1922 to 1937.

NORMIE HIMES

1933

**Normie Himes** wore this black cap when he played for the New York Americans. In 1929-'30 he recorded 50 points in 44 games.

1932

**Fifteen-thousand-seat arenas** housed NHL hockey by the 1940s, but training camps were still held in smaller Canadian cities. The Leafs prepared for the upcoming season in St. Catharines, Ontario.

1941

1946

**The Boston Bruins, Stanley Cup champions, 1928-29.** *Front row,* left to right: Tiny Thompson, Frank Fredrickson, Eddie Shore, Lionel Hitchman, Cy Denneny, Dutch Gainor, Hal Winkler. *Back row:* Cooney Weiland, Harry Oliver, Eric Pettinger, Dit Clapper, Lloyd Klein, Perk Galbraith, Eddie Hodden, Red Green.

**The steady addition of good, young players** to complement talented veterans enabled the Bruins to finish first in the NHL's American division each year from 1928 to 1931. Hitchman and Shore were two of the league's best defenders, and, beginning in 1929, the "Dynamite Line" of Clapper, Weiland and Gainor began to produce for Boston. In 1930 they combined for 102 goals and 81 assists.

"A lot of people don't know that I once played with Boston. In the 1920s, I played for Vancouver in an exhibition series in the East against Boston. Then we went out to the coast and I played for Boston against Vancouver for two or three games. But nobody knows that!" — *King Clancy*

**Dit Clapper, right, was the first NHLer to play 20 years** in the league — all with Boston. He was a successful right winger, but became a six-time all-star later in his career when he was shifted back to defense. In the mid-'40s he served the Bruins in the dual capacity of playing coach.

1940

**The 1940 New York Rangers** set an
NHL record, playing their first 19
games of the regular schedule
without a loss. They battled with the
Bruins throughout the schedule,
finally losing first place in the
standings after a 2-1 loss in front of
more than 16,000 noisy fans in
Boston. Ranger goaltender Dave
Kerr allowed only 77 goals over 48
games and continued to play well
during the playoffs.

The Rangers' Cup-winning team
featured brothers Neil and Mac
Colville who played with Alex
Shibicky on New York's top scoring
line.

Ranger manager Lester Patrick,
top right, assured himself of a place
in hockey's stock of legends when, at
the age of 44, he played in place of
his team's injured goaltender.

Sugar Jim Henry, right, broke into
the NHL in 1941 with the Rangers.
Here he stops Boston star Milt
Schmidt. The Bruins and Rangers
were great rivals in the NHL's
American division.

1928

1941

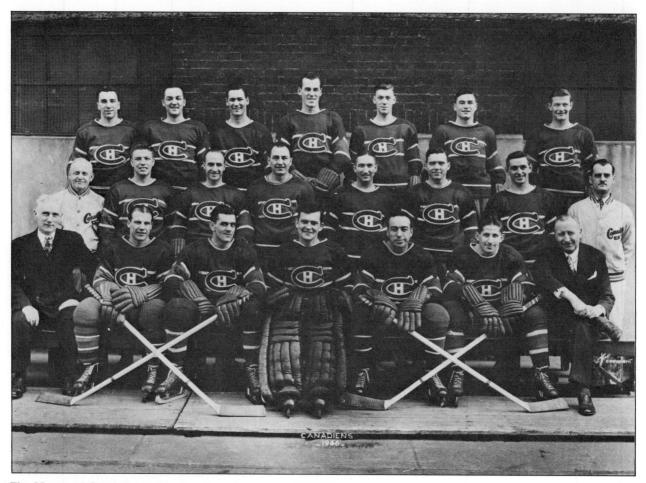

**The Montreal Canadiens, Stanley Cup champions, 1945-'46.**
*Front row,* left to right: Dick Irvin, Glen Harmon, Rocket Richard, Bill Durnan, Toe Blake, Elmer Lach, Tommy Gorman; *Second row:* E. Cook, Frankie Eddolls, Billy Reay, Joe Benoit, Dutch Hiller, Buddy O'Connor, Gerry Plamondon, Hector Dubois; *Top row:* Bob Fillion, Leo Lamoureux, Jimmy Peters, Butch Bouchard, Kenny Mosdell, Ken Reardon, Murph Chamberlain.

**"By 1946, the Punch Line** [made up of Richard, Blake and Lach] was flying. Bill Durnan was at his best in goal and Kenny Reardon, having just come back from the war, was strong on defense. Murph "Hardrock" Chamberlain [opposite, bottom], Jimmy Peters and Ken Mosdell were terrific diggers and checkers. This is when the Canadiens started to get going. Mr. Frank Selke became managing director in the summer of 1946, and it was from these players and the institution of many farm clubs, that the team really started to produce." — *Camil DesRoches*

1945

"**I saw Rocket Richard** [above, center] break his leg the first year he played for the Canadiens in 1942-'43. He was a young player who nobody knew too much about. He had scored two goals that night against Frankie Brimsek, giving him five for the year, when he was hit and fell straight to the ice. He was unable to play again that year. He had also broken a leg playing senior hockey and many people thought that he was simply too brittle and would never make it."
— *Dick Irvin*

Two seasons later, Richard had become hockey's most potent scorer.

c. 1946

1958

# THE BIG SIX: 1947 TO 1967

**"This is the first day of training camp.** Sid Abel, in his first year as head coach, has his back to the camera. I'm standing at about two o'clock on the circle. [General manager] Jack Adams is in the center. After a skate, he'd gather us together and lay down the rules. Sixty players would come to camp every year. Twenty would go to Indianapolis, twenty to Omaha and twenty would make Detroit. I can hear Jack Adams: 'Nobody's job is secure. Gentlemen, there are seven jobs in question.' And I'd think 'Oh, oh.'" — *Gordie Howe*

1947

**Toronto players react** as Syl Apps' overtime goal gives the Leafs a 3-1 edge in games in the final series. Canadiens' publicity director Camil DesRoches, at left, in street clothes, mirrors opposite emotions.

c. 1950

**"At the end of the second period** in a big game against Toronto, the score was tied. My dad [Dick Irvin, Sr.] went into the dressing room and offered $100 to the player scoring the winning goal. Normie Dussault scored it, and here's my dad paying off [right]. Conn Smythe complained that this was illegal, though I'm sure he would have done the same thing. I can hear NHL president Clarence Campbell: 'The money was offered simply as a well-done award.'"
— *Dick Irvin, Jr.*

1950

c. 1955

**Floyd Curry and Bert Olmstead** look for a loose puck in front of goaltender Terry Sawchuk. Kneeling at right is defenseman Bob Goldham.

"Sawchuk was the best goalie I ever saw. In the early 1950s he used to amaze me. I couldn't believe how he could go down on the ice and get up so quickly. One night he played a game in Montreal and the shots were 43 to 12 in favor of the Canadiens, and the Red Wings won the game 3-1. They didn't have to clean the ice in the Canadiens' end between periods because the play was all in the Detroit zone. The Canadiens used to get up so high to play Detroit and Sawchuk used to beat them by himself. No goalie impressed me like he did until Bernie Parent with the Philadelphia Flyers in their two Cup-winning seasons of 1974 and 1975." — *Dick Irvin*

1949

**Tod Sloan challenges** goaltender Bill Durnan, as Glen Harmon, left, and Rip Riopelle pursue.

1950

1949

1950

"**Bill Durnan** [top] and Turk Broda [center] were the two best goalies of their time on the two best teams of the 1940s. Durnan was the more successful during the season; Broda the more successful in the playoffs."
— *Ken Dryden*

"Durnan was the only goalie who used to switch hands on the stick and catch with either hand. His hands were naturally padded — almost like baby fat — but in practice he'd conserve himself. The skaters used to bet among themselves who would score on him and he used to make them mad by sometimes not trying very hard to stop them.

According to Rocket Richard, Frank Brimsek [bottom] was the toughest goalie he ever faced. He was called 'Mr. Zero,' having recorded six shutouts in his first eight games. He was from Minnesota iron country, where many of the first US-born NHL players were born."
— *Dick Irvin*

1952

"**Former NHL coach Fred Shero has a story** about Billy Mosienko [above] who holds the record for scoring three goals in 21 seconds. After his NHL days were over, Mosienko and Shero played for the Winnipeg Warriors. While killing a penalty, a Winnipeg player scored two goals in fourteen seconds. Alf Pike, the coach, was going to change lines and Mosienko, who was on the bench, said, 'Leave him on. He's got a chance to break my record.' Shero claims the guy hit the post." — *Dick Irvin*

1948

**In Gordie Howe's splendid professional career,** he played in the NHL over five different decades. The 1948-'49 season saw him win his first of 21 all-star team selections as a 20-year-old with the Detroit Red Wings. Beginning in the playoffs of that season, he emerged as a top scorer. From 1950 to 1953, when NHL defenses allowed the fewest goals-per-game of any era, he scored more than 40 goals each year.

**The 1949 NHL All-Star Team** First row, from left: Ken Reardon, Sid Abel, Bill Durnan, Chuck Rayner, Bob Goldham, Roy Conacher; second row: Tommy Ivan, Jack Stewart, Tony Leswick, Paul Ronty, Maurice Richard, Bill Quackenbush, Gordie Howe, Clarence Campbell; third row: trainer, Billy Mosienko, Glen Harmon, Ted Lindsay, Buddy O'Connor, Edgar Laprade, Doug Bentley, Pat Egan.

**"The Russians started playing hockey** in 1947. This is the Red Army team in that first year. In 1949 a Czech team, LTC Prague, went to Russia and showed them what real hockey was all about. I believe they left their equipment behind. You can see in this photo that the players have no padding, no shoulder harness and are probably using rolled-up newspaper as shin guards. They're not even wearing tube skates. Third and second from the right are Anatoly Tarasov and Vsevolod Bobrov, who went on to be two of the top coaches of the Russian national team." — *George Gross*

1947

1958

**Harry Sinden played** for the Whitby Dunlops' world-championship senior team in 1958. He later coached and managed the NHL's Boston Bruins.

"Viktor Konavalenko [above, right] played goal for the USSR against Canada in the 1955 world-championship final in West Germany. Canada was represented by the Penticton V's, who beat the Russians 5-0. The V's had a defenseman named George McAvoy who hit the Russians top center, Vsevolod Bobrov, so hard that I thought he was going to hit the time clock. That finished Bobrov."
— *George Gross*

Upsets in hockey often involve spectacular goaltending. Jack McCartan, right, led the US Olympic hockey team to a gold medal in 1960.

1960

1959

c. 1950

1946

**In addition** to high-quality amateur hockey, each NHL team sponsored junior and minor pro clubs. New York Ranger Edgar Laprade, top, starred with the 1939 Port Arthur (Ontario) Bearcats, one of Canada's best senior amateur clubs.
Gump Worsley, first row, center, also became a Ranger, playing junior hockey with the Verdun Cyclones in Quebec.

**Toronto's Maple Leaf captain Teeder Kennedy** greets then-Princess Elizabeth in Maple Leaf Gardens. Leaf Dick Duff and a New York player show less decorum in the penalty box.

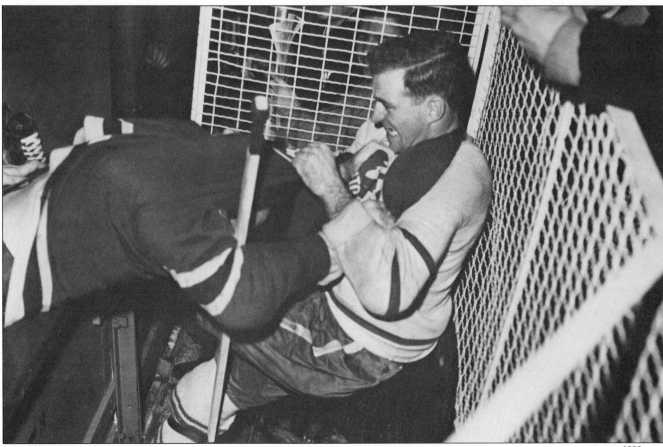

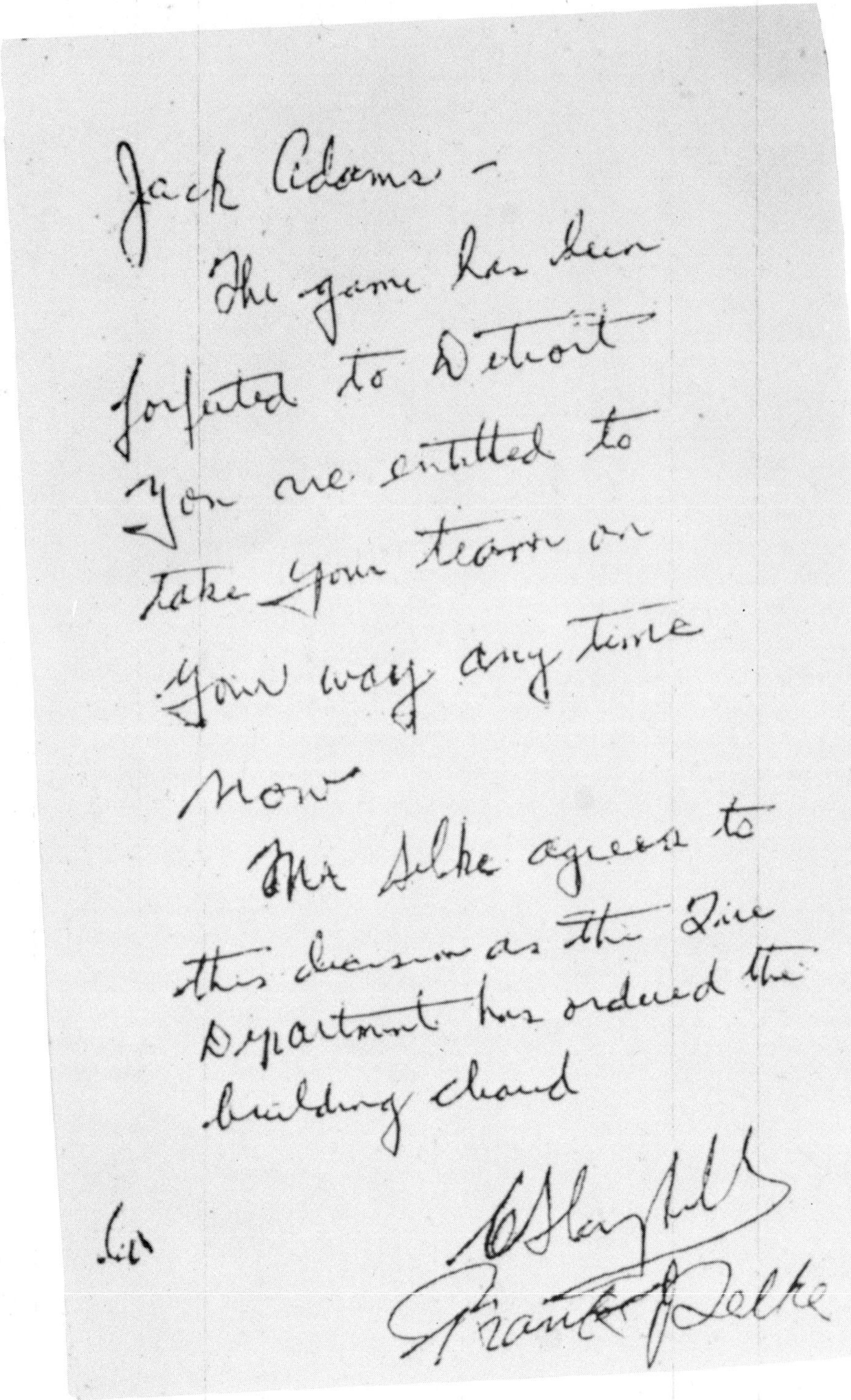

Jack Adams —

The game has been
forfeited to Detroit
You are entitled to
take your team on
your way any time
now

Mr Selke agrees to
this decision as the Fire
Department has ordered the
building cleared

*Campbell*
*Frank J. Selke*

1955

**NHL president Clarence Campbell wrote this note,** which informed Detroit general manager Jack Adams that the Montreal Forum was being cleared and that the March 17, 1955, game between Montreal and Detroit was forfeited to the Red Wings. The unruly crowd in the Forum, protesting the suspension of their star scorer, Rocket Richard, spilled into downtown Montreal to stage what has become known as the Richard Riot.

"**There is no explosive player** in hockey today to compare with Maurice 'Rocket' Richard."
— *George Gross*

"**When the Rocket hit** the opponent's blueline with the puck, he would, if he had to, go through a brick wall. He was so physically strong. He had to be, to score goals with a checker draped on his back. He wanted to win and loved to score." — *Jean Beliveau*

"**The Rocket's determination** and dedication were so great that he knew only one thing: score goals."
— *Danny Gallivan*

c. 1953

1954

**In alone,** Richard scores his first of the season against Chicago's Al Rollins.

1950

**"This is one of my favorite pictures.** We were called the Production Line. We used to pose for photographs on the assembly lines in the big Detroit auto plants. Our line ended up 1-2-3 in scoring in 1949-'50, which was a great accomplishment. There were cash awards for finishing first and second only, so rather than fight for it, we agreed to split it three ways. Sid Abel [middle] used to say that he was 'The Thinker' who had to motivate me and slow Ted Lindsay [right] down. We never started a year as a unit. They'd always split us up at the beginning trying to spread the scoring around, but we'd end up together." — *Gordie Howe*

**"Ted Lindsay had a lot of heart.** He wasn't big, but he played tough every night. Abel was very smooth at center. He could lay in that beautiful pass. They had what every scoring line needs: somebody [Abel] who could set up the play, Lindsay working hard along the boards and a great scorer in Gordie on the other side. To me, Gordie is the best all-around hockey player I've ever seen. He was astonishingly fast and strong as well as being proud of his team and his ability. I'm proud to have played my 18 years in the NHL against him." — *Jean Beliveau*

**"The rivalry** between Detroit and the Canadiens in the 1950s was fantastic. Detroit finished first seven years in a row between 1949 and 1955. We had many, many great games against them in the Forum and the old Detroit Olympia." — *Jean Beliveau*

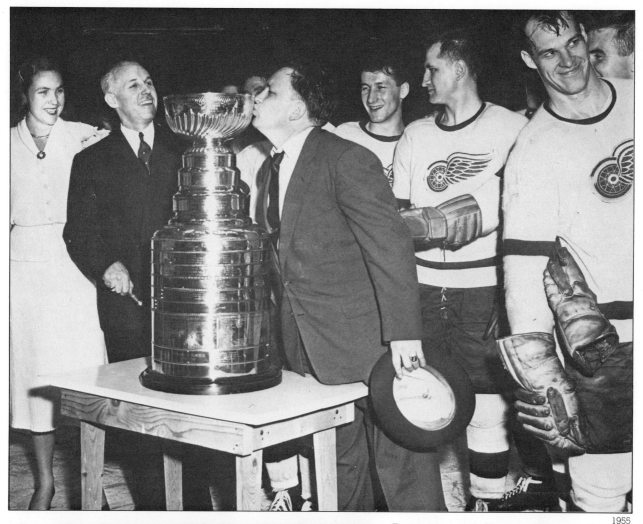

1955

**Detroit coach Jimmy Skinner** kisses the Cup after the Red Wings' 3-1 seventh-game win against Montreal. The Canadiens played without Rocket Richard, whose suspension in March provoked the "Richard Riot" (see page 126). Detroit won the Stanley Cup four times between 1950 and 1955.

1959

**Over 26 years in the NHL,** injuries forced Gordie Howe to miss only 57 regular-season games.

1960

**Gordie Howe, wearing a helmet** because of a minor injury, concentrates on controlling the puck in front of goalie Cesare Maniago. Allan Stanley, sprawling, and Tim Horton defend for the Leafs. Vic Stasiuk (11) and Gerry Melnyk (14) look for a pass.

**GORDIE HOWE NIGHT**
MARCH 3, 1959
OLYMPIA STADIUM . . . DETROIT  **25¢**

1954

**Detroit needed all seven games** of the final to defeat the Montreal Canadiens and win the Stanley Cup in 1954.

Above, goalie Terry Sawchuk is kneeling at the Cup in front of coach Tommy Ivan. Two players to the right of Ivan and facing the camera is Tony Leswick, whose screened shot deflected off Montreal defenseman Doug Harvey to give Detroit the win in overtime.

The Detroit-Montreal rivalry continues at right, as goalie Gerry McNeil tries to cover the short side against Red Wing Earl "Dutch" Reibel. Bernie Geoffrion (5) and Doug Harvey look on.

1955

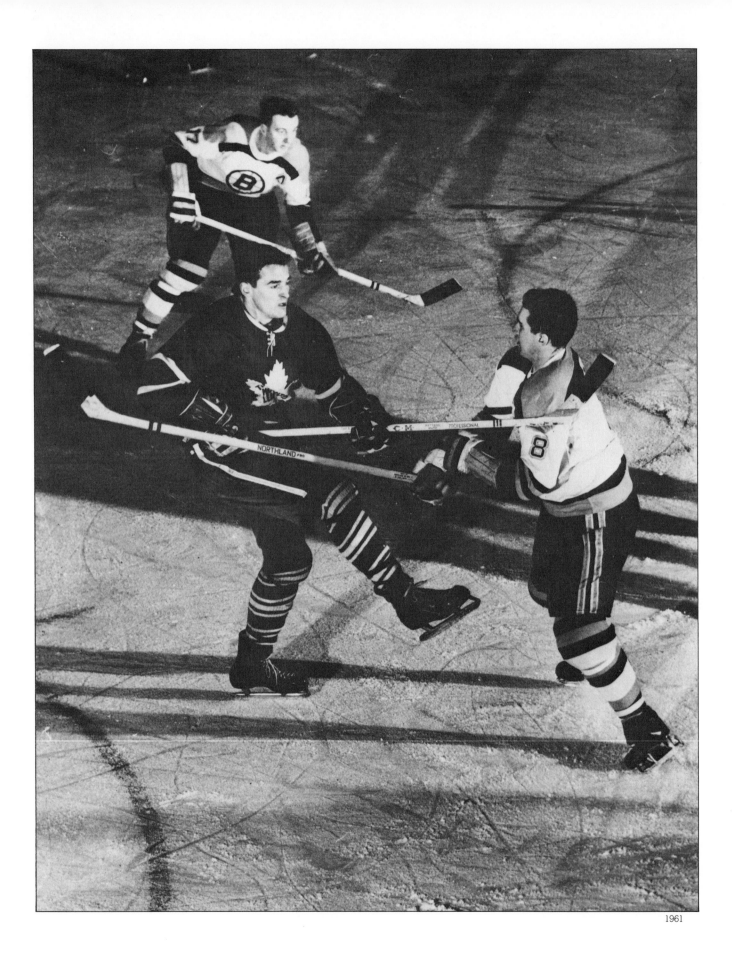

1961

c. 1957

**Toronto's Frank Mahovlich,** in the midst of a 48-goal season, fences with Boston defenseman Dallas Smith.

"If Leaf fans recall the great Toronto teams of the 1950s and '60s, they probably have a feeling of disappointment in themselves about the way they reacted to Frank Mahovlich. Today, when Frank goes to a game or plays in an old-timers' game, the crowd reacts more warmly to him than to any other player announced. You can sense that feeling of trying to make it up, but of course they can't. He was an outstanding player for the Leafs, and a rival to Bobby Hull, but the fans in Toronto never forgave him for not being the kind of game-breaking player that Hull was." — *Ken Dryden*

**Henri Richard played on a record** 11 Stanley Cup winners in 20 seasons with Montreal. Though his style differed from that of his brother, the Rocket, they shared a love of winning.

1959

**Boom-Boom Geoffrion** scoring on Boston's Don Simmons.

**Super-checker Claude Provost,** shown with coach Toe Blake, opposite page, top, "covered the other team's top scorers and almost made them powerless. He did it all by skating and almost never took a penalty. He was never intentionally mean or dirty. He took a lot of pleasure in doing the job the team asked of him." — *Camil DesRoches*

**In 1961 the Chicago Black Hawks** ended Montreal's five-year hold on the Stanley Cup with a strong team built around goalie Glenn Hall, defenseman Pierre Pilote and forwards Bobby Hull and Stan Mikita. At right, Hull, wearing number 16, is joined by Jack Evans.

1958

1961

1965

**Roger Crozier**

**Terry Sawchuk leaves his crease** to clear the puck away from an onrushing Claude Provost.

1963

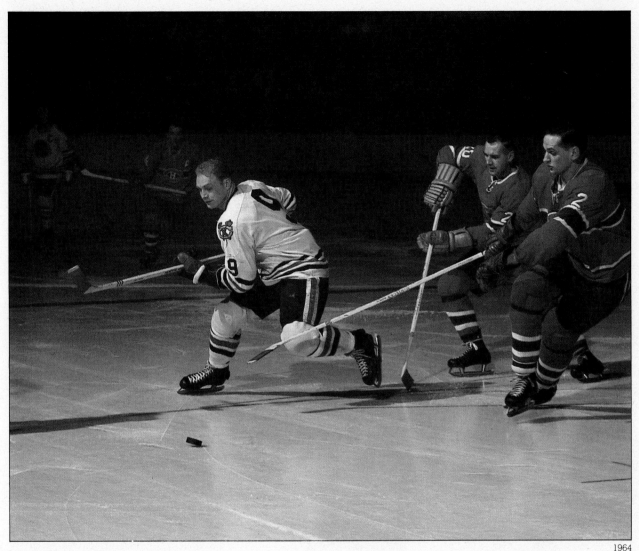

1964

**Dave Balon (20) and Jacques Laperriere (2)** check Bobby Hull in a game played in Montreal.

**Bobby Hull was the first player** to surpass Rocket Richard's record of 50 goals in a season with 54 of his own in 1965-'66.

"Hull was a lightning-fast skater with an absolutely brutal slapshot. No matter where he went, he created excitement." — *George Gross*

"The first time he ever appeared on the ice with the Chicago Black Hawks was when my dad was coaching the team in 1955-'56 at its training camp in Welland, Ontario. My dad couldn't get on skates because he was ill. He used to hire players, usually minor-leaguers, to drop the puck and referee the practice games. One day the guy who was supposed to do this didn't show up and a young blond kid in the front row who was there for the junior training camp said, 'I'll do it!' He got his skates, went out there with the pros and was in complete command." — *Dick Irvin*

c. 1962
**Pierre Pilote (3) was chosen** as the NHL's top defenseman in 1962, '63 and '64.

**The Chicago Black Hawks** finished sixth and last nine times in the 11 years immediately following World War II. But the arrival of talented young players rebuilt the club and, with a Stanley Cup win in 1961, the Hawks established themselves as one of the better teams in the league.

Despite great goaltending from Glenn Hall and a potent offense led by Hull and Mikita, Chicago was unable to win another championship with the nucleus of players that won in 1961. The team reached the finals twice more before expansion, losing to Toronto in 1962 and Montreal in 1965.

1963

**Elmer Vasko (4), with puck,** was the defense partner of Pierre Pilote on the Black Hawks' teams of the early '60s. He was one of the biggest players in the NHL, at six feet, three inches and 220 pounds, earning him the nickname "Moose." Vasko, like many of the Hawks, was coached by Rudy Pilous both as a junior in St. Catharines, Ontario, and as a professional when Pilous moved up to the Hawks in 1957.

1965

**Detroit defeated the New York Rangers 4-1** in this game in Madison Square Garden. Goaltender Jacques Plante joined the Rangers from Montreal when the two clubs swapped goaltenders before the start of the 1964 season. This trade, which sent Gump Worsley to the Canadiens, demonstrated that goaltending is only one part of successful defensive hockey. Before the trade, Plante's goals-against average was approximately three-quarters of a goal per game better than Worsley's. After changing teams, this was reversed, as Worsley had the benefit of Montreal's strong defense in front of him.

The success enjoyed by the Montreal Canadiens in the 1950s and '60s was based on scoring punch combined with puck-controlling defense. Jean-Guy Talbot played 12 seasons on defense for Montreal, paired with Doug Harvey, Dollard St. Laurent, Bob Turner, Terry Harper, J.C. Trembley, Jacques Laperriere and others.

These three photographs, all taken during the same game in Toronto in 1961, illustrate how a good defenseman involves himself in a constant battle to control the puck and check opposing players in his own end. Talbot, working behind the Canadiens' net, is challenged by Dave Keon, top, Frank Mahovlich, center, and Eddie Shack, bottom.

1966

**Rookie sensation Bobby Orr** circles behind Johnny Bower.

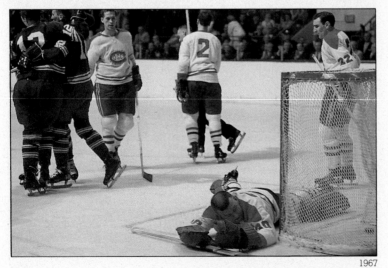

1967

**Johnny Bower reached the NHL** after 13 years in the minors. He was the number one goaltender for the Leafs when Toronto won three consecutive Stanley Cups in 1962, '63 and '64. Beginning with the 1965-'66 season, he shared the position with Terry Sawchuk, as these two veterans became the first co-winners of the Vezina Trophy.

Jim Pappin's second-period goal, at left, proved to be the Cup-winner, as Toronto won the last Stanley Cup awarded in the NHL's six-team era.

1961

**Toronto's defense was tailor-made**
for playoff hockey. Tim Horton (7),
above, Bob Baun, right, Allan
Stanley, Red Kelly and Carl Brewer
were all-star defensemen.

Baun broke his leg late in the sixth
game of the 1964 finals. He had it
taped, enabling him to stay in the
game and score the winner in
overtime. "He didn't go to the
hospital until after the seventh game.
I went with him and saw X-rays that
revealed a cracked fibula. Only a
player of Baun's stature could have
played with such pain."
—*George Gross*

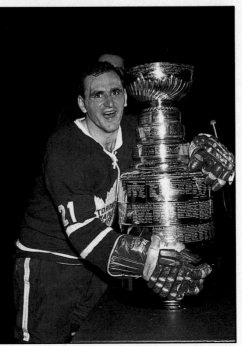

1964

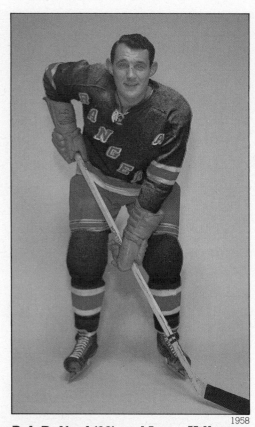

1958

1965

**Bob Pulford (20) and Larry Hillman**
tie up Phil Esposito in front of Toronto
goaltender Terry Sawchuk, at right.
Esposito began his remarkable NHL
career with Chicago in 1963. He was
used as a playmaking center, feeding
Bobby Hull, who led the league in
goals scored in 1966 and 1967.

Esposito's strength on his skates
enabled him to position himself in
front of the opposition's net, looking
to deflect shots or bang in rebounds.

The 1967 trade that sent Esposito
to the Boston Bruins marked his
emergence as one of the most
proficient centermen in the NHL. He
was selected to the NHL all-star team
in each of his first eight years in
Boston.

Bill Gadsby, above, played
defense for 20 seasons in the NHL
with Chicago, New York and Detroit.

**Bobby Orr listens to coach Harry Sinden** at the Boston superstar's first NHL training camp in September 1966. Orr was widely heralded as a game-breaking player who had dominated every game he played as a junior with the Oshawa Generals of the Ontario Hockey Association. The long-suffering Bruins needed new talent, and in Orr they found themselves a player who was a master of the sport.

New York Ranger Harry Howell won the Norris Trophy as the NHL's best defenseman in Orr's rookie year. Accepting the award he said, "I'm glad I won this now, because there's a young man coming along who is sure to win for many years to come." Howell's prediction was accurate. Orr won the award in each of the next eight seasons.

In this photograph, he has yet to be assigned the uniform number 4 that he would soon make famous.

1967

# EXPANSION: 1968 TO DATE

**Professional hockey began to change** in 1967 as the NHL added six new teams. By 1972, a rival league competed for talent, and open international series demonstrated the high quality of play in Europe.

Bobby Orr, left, ushered in modern high-speed hockey.

**Six new teams formed a west division** of the NHL in 1967. The Philadelphia Flyers finished first in their inaugural season, followed by the Los Angeles Kings, St. Louis Blues, Minnesota North Stars, Pittsburgh Penguins and Oakland Seals. In 1968, 1969 and 1970, the Blues advanced to the Stanley Cup final where they were defeated twice by Montreal and once by Boston.

1968

"**John Ferguson** was the motivator for the Canadiens in the first years following expansion. From 1961 to 1965, we finished first three times, but couldn't get going in the playoffs because our players were too small. On the advice of Floyd Curry, we brought John Ferguson from Cleveland, and that changed the whole complexion of the team. The Canadiens won the Cup in 1965, '66, '68 and '69, and Fergie was one of the big reasons we won. Our small players felt they could go out and play with him there. He meant a lot to us and more than earned his money."
— *Camil DesRoches*

1968

Gordie Howe turned 40 near the
end of the 1967-'68 season in which
he recorded 39 goals and earned a
berth on the all-star team. The
following year, Detroit acquired
former Toronto star Frank Mahovlich
who played left wing on a line with
Howe and center Alex Delvecchio.
Howe had 44 goals and 59 assists for
a total of 103 points—his personal
best in the NHL.

The Buffalo Sabres emerged as
one of the NHL's top clubs in their
fifth season, 1974-'75. The French
Connection line of Rick Martin, Gil
Perrault and René Robert led them to
the Stanley Cup finals. At right,
Montreal's Ken Dryden clears the
puck away from Rick Martin.

1975

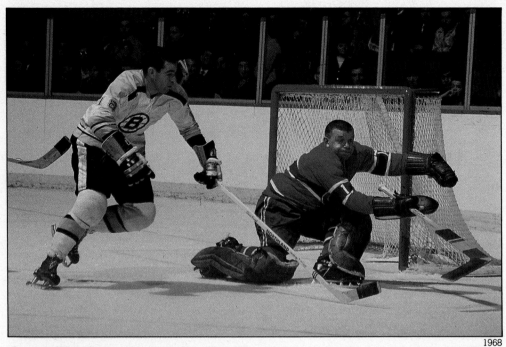

1968

**Gump Worsley** played goal on four Cup-winners for Montreal in the 1960s. Over 20 NHL seasons, he recorded 43 shutouts and a goals-against average of 2.91 per game.

**Tony Esposito**, bottom, recorded 15 shutouts in 1969-'70, his first full season in the NHL.

**"Gerry Cheevers** [right] was every bit as much the Bruins' on-ice leader as Bobby Orr was in the 1970's."
—*Fran Rosa*

1971

1978

1975

1976

**The Philadelphia Flyers** were the "Broad Street Bullies" who dominated the NHL for two seasons in the mid-1970s. Captain Bobby Clarke and goaltender Bernie Parent, opposite, were the best in the NHL at their jobs. Clarke played a fierce, hustling game and was the NHL's premier on-ice leader. Parent led the league in shutouts and goals-against in the team's two Cup-winning seasons, 1973-'74 and 1974-'75.

Bill Barber, left, was a courageous left wing whose straight-to-the-net style rewarded him with a 50-goal season and an all-star selection in 1976.

1976

1975

**"One day at Boston Garden,** Phil Esposito shouted over and asked that the gate at the players' exit be left open. 'About four or five inches,' he said. 'Watch this.' Then he skated to the blue line about 70 feet away from the door, and shot. The puck hooked left and went through the small opening, touching nothing.

   'Do it again,' I said.

   'Oh, no,' he said, and went off the ice laughing."
—*Fran Rosa*

**Two centers,** a right wing and a defenseman have dominated the NHL scoring championship since expansion in 1967. Phil Esposito won the Art Ross Trophy as the league's top scorer five times and his teammate, Bobby Orr, won it twice between 1969 and 1975. The combination of Esposito and Orr made the Bruins the most potent offensive team in the NHL and brought them the Cup in 1970 and 1972.

   Esposito registered more than 60 goals in four different seasons. His best year was 1970-'71 when, in 78 games, he established a new NHL record of 76 goals and 76 assists for 152 points. That same season, Orr set a record for assists with 102.

   Guy Lafleur, top right, was heralded as the league's most electrifying right winger for six seasons beginning in 1974-'75. He won the Art Ross Trophy in 1976, 1977 and 1978, and scored 50 or more goals every year from 1975 to 1980.

   In his first season in the NHL, Wayne Gretzky, bottom right, finished in a tie with Marcel Dionne as the NHL's top point-getter. The Art Ross Trophy has been Gretzky's alone since 1980. He became the first NHL player to score more than 200 points in a single season with 212 in 1981-'82.

1977

**"Wayne Gretzky is amazing.** There is so much hooking and interference in today's hockey, but he has an ability to put himself in the clear, even against close checking. It's his great hockey sense." —*Jean Beliveau*

"Wayne is a perfectionist who is blessed with the gift of total concentration." —*Gordie Howe*

1983

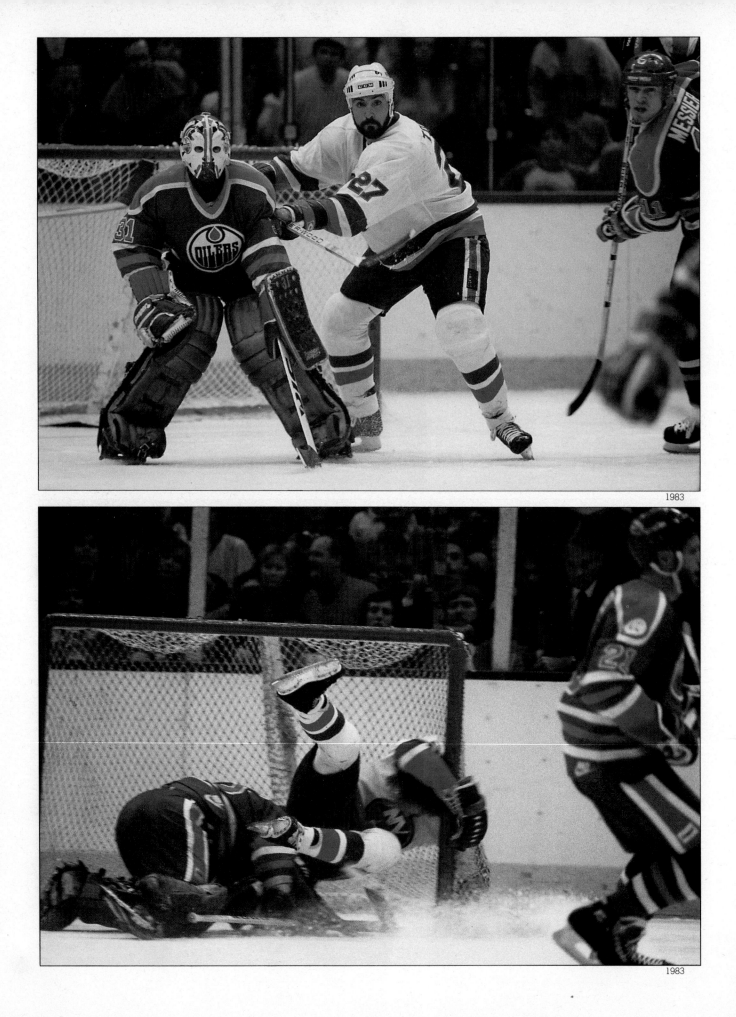

1983

1983

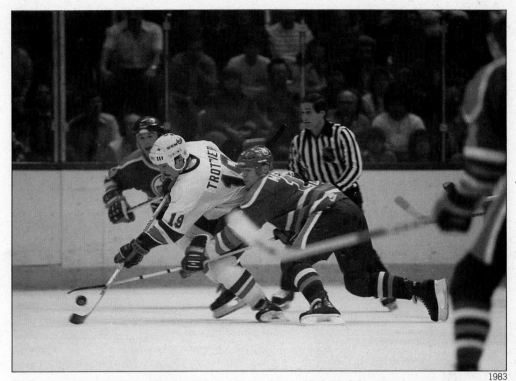

1983

**Two superlative forwards:** Bryan Trottier and Mark Messier.

**The Edmonton Oilers and New York Islanders** met in the Stanley Cup final in two successive seasons. The Islanders won the first of these meetings four games to none in 1983, giving them four straight championships. The following season, the improved Oilers defeated the Islanders in five games.

John Tonelli, opposite top, works for position against Oiler goalie Grant Fuhr. Tonelli's digging style was rewarded when he was selected as the most valuable player in the 1984 Canada Cup international tournament.

Fast-skating Bob Nystrom, opposite bottom, is upset into the Edmonton net. Nystrom scored the overtime Cup-winning goal in 1980, the Islanders' first championship season.

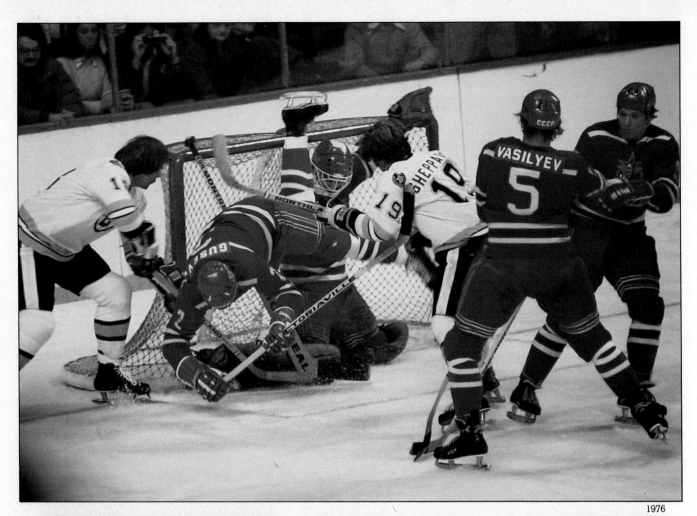

1976

1973

**The Soviet player** who most captivated the imaginations of North American fans was Vladislav Tretiak. As goaltender for the Red Army and the Soviet Nationals through the 1970s, Tretiak repeatedly turned back the best scoring efforts of international and NHL all-stars.

1975

**"The 3-3 New Year's Eve tie** between the Canadiens and Red Army was an almost-perfect game."
— *Camil DesRoches*

**Team Canada,** made up of NHL players, celebrates a last-minute goal by Paul Henderson in the eighth game of what came to be known as the "Super Series." This first confrontation between NHL pros and the Soviets was tied after seven games, both teams having won three and tied one.

   "This is my only recollection of the third period. I don't remember the goals being scored. I can remember two things: racing down the ice to get into this pile-up and then, just at the moment this picture was taken, suddenly thinking to myself, 'There are 34 seconds to go! I've got to get a hold of myself. It's not over.' " — *Ken Dryden*

**"The 1980 US gold** medal proves what nationalism, heart and guts can do when combined with inspired coaching. It convinces a bunch of college players that they're superstars." — *George Gross*

**The US National Team,** gold-medal winners, 1980 Olympics. *Front row,* left to right: Steve Janaszak, Bill Baker, Mark Johnson, Craig Patrick, Mike Eruzione, Herb Brooks, Buzz Schneider, Jack O'Callahan, Jim Craig. *Second row:* Bob Suter, Rob McClanahan, Mark Wells, B. Kessel, V.G. Nagobads, G. Smith, R.W. Fleming, R. Jasinski, W. Strelow, Bruce Horsch, Neal Broten, Mark Pavelich. *Top row:* Phil Verchota, Steve Christoff, Les Auge, Dave Delich, Jack Hughes, Ken Morrow, Mike Ramsey, Dave Christian, Ralph Cox, Dave Silk, John Harrington, Eric Strobel.

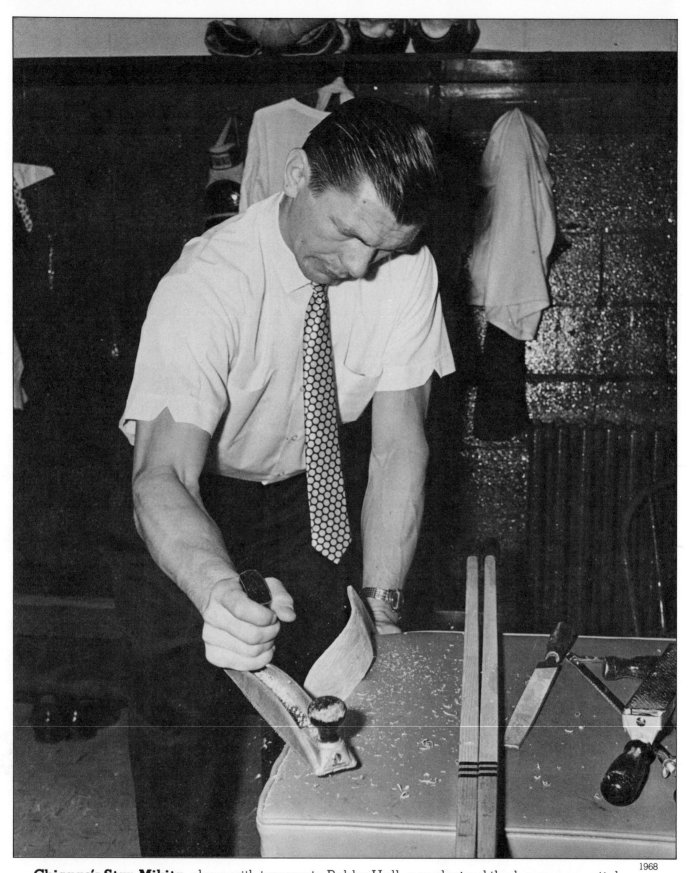

**Chicago's Stan Mikita,** along with teammate Bobby Hull, popularized the boomerang stick.

1968

**"Derek Sanderson and Bobby Orr** [right] make strange opponents after being teammates on Stanley Cup champions in Boston. Sanderson — a master at winning face-offs and a great penalty killer — was a player whose vast potential was never fully realized." — *Fran Rosa*

Jean Ratelle, 19, was briefly a Bruin and teammate of Orr, too, when, in the NHL's biggest trade of the 1970s, he went to Boston for what proved to be Orr's last season.

**The World Hockey Association** served notice that it was in business with the celebrated signing of Bobby Hull by the Winnipeg Jets in 1972. In the new league's first finals, the New England Whalers defeated the Jets four games to one. The Whalers, Jets, Quebec Nordiques and Edmonton Oilers joined the NHL after seven WHA seasons. Below, Brad Selwood jousts with Bobby Hull in the New England crease.

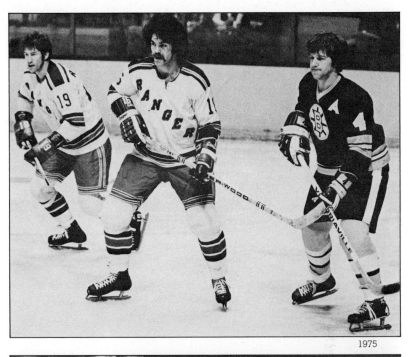

1975

1973

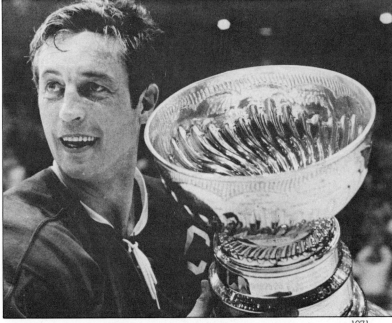

1971

**"This was my last Stanley Cup,** and we won in Chicago in seven games. Ken Dryden had joined the team in March. He gave us the goaltending you need to win in the playoffs. Our biggest upset also went to seven games, against Boston in the quarter-finals. Esposito and Orr were flying, and the Bruins were favored to win the Cup." — *Jean Beliveau*

1971

**Goalie Gerry Cheevers,** always tough in the playoffs, is guarded by Bobby Orr as Jean Beliveau looks to pass the puck.

1970

1972

**The Bruins finished last** and missed the playoffs for the eighth consecutive year in 1966-'67, Bobby Orr's first NHL season. Three years later, they won the Stanley Cup in four straight games over the St. Louis Blues. Orr, bottom left, scored the winning goal.

"This moment will be etched in the minds of Boston hockey fans forever. It was in Boston Garden, on Mother's Day, 1970. Orr had come in from the right point on a gambling move to get a pass from Derek Sanderson. Defenseman Noel Picard had flipped Orr into the air as the puck went in. The other Boston defenseman on the ice was Don Awrey, who said, 'All I could think was that if Bobby doesn't get the puck, it will be four-on-one, and I'm the one!'" — *Fran Rosa*

Orr was all-powerful on the ice, but knee injuries forced his early retirement. His last great show came in the 1976 Canada Cup international tournament, when he was named most valuable player.

"There was a night in Boston when Orr accidently put the puck in his own net. A voice from the balcony shouted, 'It's all right, Bobby. We still love you!'" —*Fran Rosa*

1975

**Rick MacLeish** was the Flyers' kind of hockey player. He combined a scoring touch with an ability to gain position in front of the opposition's net. In his first full season in Philadelphia, he had 100 points and 50 goals.

**The romance between the Philadelphia Flyers and their fans** in the mid-'70s created instant traditions in The Spectrum that rivalled those of long-established teams. Kate Smith's singing of "God Bless America" was echoed full-voice by the sellout crowd of 17,077 that attended every Flyer home game. During the playoffs, player introductions took place in darkness, as spotlights raked through the crowd and onto the ice, drawing the fans and their Flyers into one shared experience. When a Philadelphia player reached a career milestone or set a club or league record, dollar-bill-sized paper souvenirs were thrown from the upper sections of the arena to flutter down over the appreciative crowd. Each slip of paper read, "Great moments in Flyer history...You were there!"

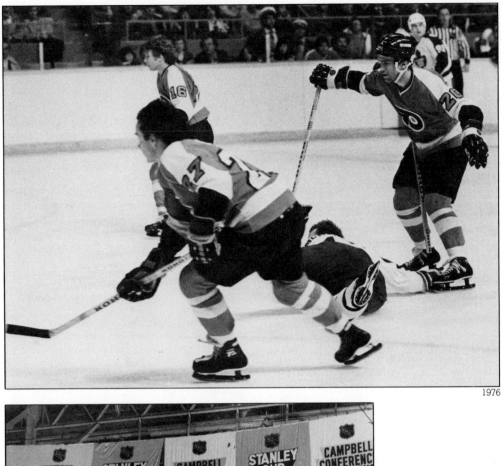

1976

1977

**Reggie Leach (27), above, blossomed as a goal scorer** with Philadelphia.
He had been the most valuable player in his junior league when, as a
linemate of Bobby Clarke, he scored 65 goals for the Flin Flon Bombers in
1970. His first four years as a professional hadn't seen him realize this
promise, but immediately upon being traded to Philadelphia in 1974, he
became a top scorer on a Stanley Cup champion. Reunited on a line with
Clarke, he had 45 goals in his first year and a league-leading 61 in his
second.

Jim Watson, (20), above, played steady defense for 10 seasons in
Philadelphia. From 1973 to 1982, the Flyers won the Cup twice and finished
first in their division on five occasions.

**Montreal centerman Jacques Lemaire** and Ranger goalie Ed Giacomin.

1974

1970

**Pete Mahovlich upended** by Bob Baun of Detroit.

**The Montreal Canadiens won four** consecutive Stanley Cups from 1976 to 1979. These Cup-winning teams balanced great scoring power with talented role players. Bob Gainey, right, with his checking ability and powerful skating style, brought new recognition to the job of the defensive forward. A Soviet hockey executive called him the "technically perfect hockey player."

1979

"Jacques Lemaire [left] was the model all-purpose player. When he first came up, he was a power-shooting left winger, but when I joined Canadiens in 1971, he was beginning to develop a new role and, for several years, was in and out of the doghouse. It was when he was made a centerman that he emerged. He has the personality and the skills of the solid, dependable, all-purpose centerman every team needs. He was a great playoff performer. You'd look at his size and his style and think that he was the kind of player who would die in the close checking of the playoffs, but he was a great competitor. He had tremendous legs and skating ability. He was almost like a cartoon character with his legs churning so fast they seemed invisible." – *Ken Dryden*

1983

**New York Islanders superb center** Bryan Trottier and Boston's Mike O'Connell concentrate on a loose puck in front of Bruin goalie Pete Peeters.

In the Islanders' first year in the NHL, 1972-'73, they finished with only 30 points and were the stereotypical first-year franchise. By their fourth season, the team had cracked the 100-point plateau, and, while the Canadiens were winning the Stanley Cup in the late '70s, continued to draft and trade wisely, building a well coached, championship-calibre team. This patience paid off in 1979-'80, as the Islanders began their own four-year string of Cup victories.

The Islanders' success was built on playmaking by Trottier, the scoring touch of Mike Bossy (22), opposite, great goaltending from Billy Smith, and a tough defense led by captain Denis Potvin (5).

1981

1981

1981

**Mike Bossy** [top left] is one of the first of the real snipers. So much of scoring until Bossy was a volume exercise, with shot after shot. He combined speed and shooting accuracy, making goals come easily. A Bossy-type of goal doesn't require enormous time and pressure. He was crucial for the Islanders' success. Before Bossy, the Islanders were that prototypical hard-working, bang-'em-around and bang-'em-at-the-net type of team. After Bossy, they didn't need sixteen minutes of sustained pressure to get a goal. Bossy could get it another way."
— *Ken Dryden*

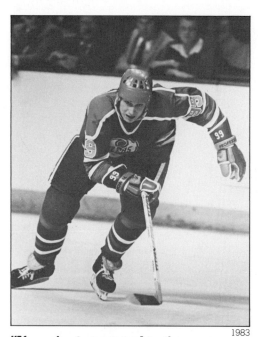

1983

**"If you're interested** in the techniques of good hockey, and don't worry about who's winning the game, you can just study the art of Wayne Gretzky. He's unbelievably smart. Playing with him, you realize how great he is. [Howe and Gretzky played together in the 1979 WHA and 1980 NHL all-star games.] He reads people very, very well. If you're in trouble and can only go one way, he goes the other. He has a great pair of hands and can either shoot the puck at 100 miles per hour or make a soft, lofty pass lay down on the ice five feet away." —*Gordie Howe*

**Edmonton's first Stanley Cup win** in 1984 established Mark Messier, below right, as one of the game's best players. Throughout the playoffs, he scored pivotal goals that lifted the Oilers past their opponents.

1984

1981

**The fastest 50 goals in NHL history** were scored by Wayne Gretzky in just 39 games in 1981-'82.

"What amazes me about Gretzky is how far ahead he is not only against other teams' top scorers, but in comparison to his own linemates as well. If you look back, you'll see that when Orr was winning, Esposito was close. When Dickie Moore had the lead, Beliveau was close behind. But Gretzky is involved in 70 more goals than any other player on his team. He is such a threat on the ice that he mentally intimidates his opposition."
— *Dick Irvin*

Goalie Grant Fuhr and defenseman Paul Coffey, right, proved that the Oilers had more than just scoring punch in winning a second Stanley Cup in 1985.

1985

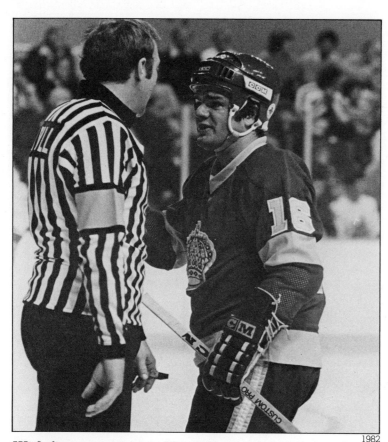

1982

**With five consecutive 50-goal seasons** coming in the midst of a steady and productive career, Marcel Dionne of the Los Angeles Kings reached the 1,000-point milestone in fewer games than any player to come before him in the NHL.

**Every NHL team** has talented players, but winning requires that talent to come together in a special and elusive way. Many splendid hockey players never come close to playing on a Cup-winner, and even the best realize that, in every athlete's career, luck — good or bad — plays its part.

"Bernie Parent was a very elegant goalie who played the position the way most goalies would like to play. He almost never seemed to be off-balance. In 1974 and 1975, he was the principle reason the Flyers won the Stanley Cup. He showed great promise as a junior, with the Bruins and with the expansion Flyers, but there seemed to be limitations. He found himself in Toronto, with Jacques Plante as his guru, but then left for the WHA and seemed destined to a career that would never go beyond being promising. But he came back to the Flyers and it was on his second turn with Philadelphia that it all worked." — *Ken Dryden*

1975

1979

# MEMORIES

**Fans, coaches, journalists, broadcasters and players** share memories of their experiences in hockey. The game leaves each of us with our own special images which, years from now, will have as much power to move us as they do today.

Here, the NHL All-Stars accept congratulations from the Soviet nationals after winning the first game of the Challenge Cup series in 1979. The Soviets won games two and three.

Many of the photographs in this book are accompanied by comments from hockey people. While the book was being prepared, selections of photographs from it were given to important players, journalists, broadcasters and hockey historians. These hockey experts studied the photographs and talked about them. Their remarks were recorded and appear here.

The National Hockey League, the publisher and the editor thank these representatives of the sport for their contributions both to hockey and to *Hockey: The Illustrated History*.

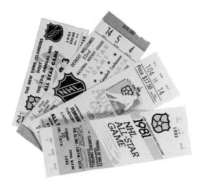

1956

c. 1933

**Jean Beliveau** became known as the most elegant of hockey players. His good looks, his smooth skating style and his one-on-one skill against opposing goaltenders made him seem almost regal on the ice.

Jean joined the Montreal Canadiens after a storied amateur career in Quebec. A sensational junior, he declined an invitation to play for the Canadiens in 1950-'51. Instead, he played two years of senior amateur hockey with the Quebec Aces, packing Le Colisée, which became known as "the house that Beliveau built." He joined the Canadiens fulltime in 1953 and, by his third season, was the NHL's scoring champion and most valuable player.

He scored 507 regular season goals and added 79 more in 17 years of playoff competition. He was a member of 10 Stanley Cup teams and was captain of the Canadiens for as many seasons.

Today he is the senior vice-president of corporate affairs for the Canadiens.

**King Clancy** was an inspirational hockey player who sparked the Ottawa Senators and the Toronto Maple Leafs for 16 seasons beginning in 1921.

He was a small and tough defenseman who played on three Stanley Cup winners. His acquisition by the Toronto Maple Leafs from Ottawa was the most celebrated hockey transaction of that era, as Toronto manager Conn Smythe parted with $35,000 and two players in return for the popular King.

Smythe's move paid off as the Leafs, with Clancy leading the defense, won the Stanley Cup in 1932.

The King went on to referee and coach in the NHL. He is an important part of the Toronto Maple Leafs today, where he's vice-president of the club.

1984

1975

**Camil DesRoches** became associated with hockey when, in 1938, Montreal Canadiens manager Tommy Gorman hired him to translate the club's English press releases into French. In 1946, when Frank Selke, Sr. became manager of the club, DesRoches was hired fulltime to head up the new publicity department.

In the ensuing years, Camil DesRoches has continued to work in the Canadiens' front office. He has become recognized as a hockey historian and expert on the Canadiens. He's currently director of special events for the Montreal Forum.

**Ken Dryden** was at the center of one of hockey's greatest upsets. In 1970-'71, the Boston Bruins had dominated the NHL regular season and were highly favored to win their second successive Stanley Cup. Montreal Canadiens' management brought up Dryden from their farm team in the last two weeks of the regular season. He played well and was given the job of stopping the spectacular offense of the Bruins.

Dryden was sensational in the playoffs, as the Canadiens defeated the Bruins in seven games, the Minnesota North Stars in six and the Chicago Black Hawks in seven to win the Stanley Cup. In the eight years he was with the Canadiens, they won the Stanley Cup six times.

Today, Dryden is Commissioner of Youth for the Province of Ontario.

1958

1978

**Danny Gallivan** is one of Canada's best known and best loved hockey broadcasters. His informed yet emotional commentary, combined with his colorful, descriptive language, established him as the voice of the Montreal Canadiens on *Hockey Night in Canada.* His voice, because of the thrilling moments it has described, has become a touchstone for hockey fans in Canada.

Now retired, Gallivan maintains an active schedule, speaking about hockey at special events across Canada and appearing on radio and television to talk about the game.

**George Gross** covered hockey for the Toronto *Telegram* newspaper from 1959 to 1971. He chronicled the Maple Leafs' Cup-winning years under Punch Imlach in the 1960s and was one of the first journalists to cover the European and international hockey scenes for both print and electronic media in Canada.

Throughout his journalistic career, Gross has worked hard to promote amateur sports and physical fitness. He is a member of the press council for the 1988 Winter Olympics in Calgary, Alberta.

Today, George Gross is the sports editor of the Toronto *Sun.*

1946

1983

**Gordie Howe** played professional hockey from 1945 to 1980. He entered the NHL a teenager and, by the time he retired, was a 52-year-old grandfather playing on the same team as his two sons.

Howe's achievements in the game surpass mere longevity. No list of the greatest hockey players of all time can exclude him, and many knowledgeable enthusiasts consider him the best to ever play the game. He has been selected as the NHL's most valuable player six times and has won the league's scoring championship on five occasions. His greatest years as a scorer coincided with the period in NHL history when defenses were strongest, allowing fewer goals-against than in any other era of the sport. It was against this tough opposition that Howe scored 43, 47, and 49 goals in three successive seasons.

Today Gordie Howe is an important member of the executive of the Hartford Whalers hockey club.

**Dick Irvin** is part of one of hockey's royal families. His father coached the Chicago Black Hawks, Toronto Maple Leafs and Montreal Canadiens for a total of 26 NHL seasons.

Irvin has established himself as one of the most proficient broadcasters covering hockey today. Working on both radio and television, Dick provides play-by-play coverage, commentary and expert analysis. He has been part of the play-by-play team that described the winning goal in 10 Stanley Cup finals.

He is the sports director of CFCF television in Montreal.

1985

c. 1955

**Fran Rosa** was sports editor of the Boston *Globe* for five years beginning in 1965 and, since 1970, has covered hockey fulltime for the newspaper. The year 1970 coincided with the Boston Bruins' first Stanley Cup win in 29 years, and Rosa was perhaps best positioned to document the glorious moments of the Orr-Esposito Bruin years.

Along with Jean Beliveau and Danny Gallivan, he sits on the Hockey Hall of Fame player selection committee and is a past-president of the Professional Hockey Writers' Association.

**Lou and Nat Turofsky** photographed many of hockey's greatest moments from the 1920s to the 1960s. Lou, left, purchased Toronto's Alexandra Studio in 1909 and took his brother, Nat, into partnership. They established their reputation as sports photographers when, in 1919, they journeyed to Chicago to cover what later turned out to be the infamous "Black Sox" World Series scandal.

The Turofskys had the ability to anticipate action, enabling them to capture the perfect moment at any sporting event. In addition to hockey, they covered rugby, boxing, baseball, lacrosse and numerous other sports.

Many of the most exciting photographs in this book come from the Turofsky archives. This important record is being preserved through the kindness of Imperial Oil Limited which purchased the Turofsky collection and donated it to the Hockey Hall of Fame.

1958

**Maurice "Rocket" Richard**

# ACKNOWLEDGMENTS

Many, many people contributed to the preparation of *Hockey: The Illustrated History.* Thanks to: Denis Brodeur, Dennis Buden of the Hartford Whalers, Vince Casey of the New York Rangers, Dean Cooke, Bill Gallaway, Stu Hackel, John Halligan, Terry Hancey, Greig Henderson, Ian Hutchinson, Claude Mouton of the Montreal Canadiens, John Neale, Ron Peter, Gwyneth Runnings, Julie Russel, Steve Ryan, Denise Schon, John To, Wendy Trueman, Paul Williams, the estate of Jack Adams, and the marketing and public relations committee of the board of governors of the NHL.

Special thanks to Carol McLaughlin.

For Nicholas and Jason in loving memory of Vivian.

## Photo credits

Amateur Hockey Association of the United States, 161

David Bier, 44, 133

Bruce Bennett, 57, 153-159

Boston Bruins, 170

CJAD Television, 182 right

Canada Wide Feature Services, 37

Ralph Dinger collection, 7, 8

Edmonton Oilers, 172

Graphic Artists, 29, 162

Terry Hancey/Masterfile, 150, 151 top, 160

Hartford Whalers, 61

The Hockey Hall of Fame collection, 2, 3, 10, 12, 19, 20, 21, 23, 31, 45, 55, 65, 66, 67, 68 top, 69, 70, 71, 73, 74, 80-85, 87, 90, 97-104, 116, 119, 120, 128, 129 top, 131, 136, 163, 164 top, 165, 167, 174-175, 182 left, 186

International Sports Properties, 123 top right

Montreal Canadiens, 179 left, 180

Bob Mummery, 173 bottom

New York Rangers, 25, 49, 91 top left, 95, 96 bottom, 106-109, 123 bottom, 124, 125 bottom, 127, 134, 168, 176-177

New York Islanders, 171

Notman Archives, McCord Museum, McGill University, 68 bottom

Frank Prazak, 39, 137-142, 144, 145 top, 146-149, 151 bottom, 152

La Presse, Montreal, 30

Public Archives of Canada, 17

Robert Shaver, 166

Toronto Sun, 181 right

The Imperial Oil Turofsky collection, 5, 14-15, 22, 28, 33, 41, 47, 49, 72, 75, 77, 79, 89, 92, 93, 105, 111, 114-115, 117, 118, 121, 125 top, 127, 129 bottom, 130, 132, 143, 145 bottom, 179 right, 183 right, 184

United Press International, 54

Wide World Photos, 164 bottom, 173 top

1960

**Cyclone Taylor** and **Foster Hewitt** break ground at the site of the Hockey Hall of Fame in Toronto.

The Hockey Hall of Fame is an important and active organization dedicated to preserving the living history of the sport. Artifacts and images of yesterday's hockey are precious and finite. The Hall of Fame and its staff do all they can to acquire and catalog these items, forming a research and information center dedicated to the game of hockey.

The editor and publisher thank the staff of the Hockey Hall of Fame for their patience and interest in this book. Special thanks to: M.H. "Lefty" Reid, Joseph Romain, Ralph Dinger and Ray Paquet.

# INDEX

Page numbers refer to text and photo captions only. Where an individual appears in a photograph without being named in the accompanying caption, no index reference is given.

c. 1956

1931

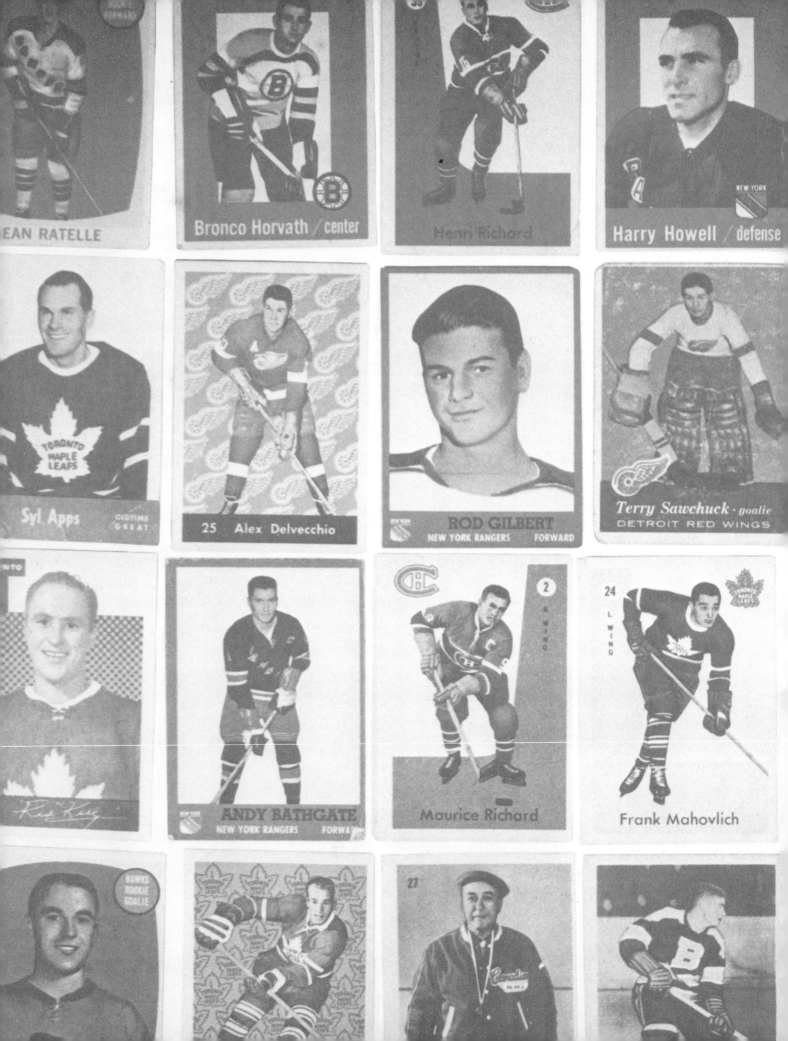

EAN RATELLE

Bronco Horvath / center

Henri Richard

Harry Howell / defense

Syl Apps        OLDTIME GREAT

25   Alex Delvecchio

ROD GILBERT
NEW YORK RANGERS        FORWARD

Terry Sawchuck · goalie
DETROIT RED WINGS

ANDY BATHGATE
NEW YORK RANGERS        FORWA

Maurice Richard

Frank Mahovlich